Tales From Four Towns

Death, Destruction, Crime and Notable News from 19th Century Walsall, Wednesbury, West Bromwich and Wolverhampton.

THE "BLACK COUNTRY."

Tales From Four Towns

Death, Destruction, Crime and Notable News from 19th Century Walsall, Wednesbury, West Bromwich and Wolverhampton.

Paul Robinson

Published by Penk Publishing

penk.publishing@gmail.com

2013

Copyright © 2013 by Paul Robinson

All rights reserved. Paul Robinson has asserted his right to be identified as the author of this work. This book may not be reproduced in whole or in part, by any means, without the express written permission of the author.

ISBN: 978-1-291-64971-0

For my wife, Joanne

Contents

Introduction..9
Explosions, Fire and Pestilence..11
Accidents, Collapses and Freak Weather.................................33
Recreation and Rip-Off..55
Misdemeanours and Mayhem..72
Murder, Misfortune and Misery...100
Addendum...132

Introduction

With their heavy industries, extensive mining operations and burgeoning populations, Walsall, Wednesbury, West Bromwich and Wolverhampton generated a wealth of news of all sorts during the nineteenth century. Being before the age of radio, newspapers were the only "mass media" available to spread this news to the population at large.

By the latter half of the century, aided by the railways, an efficient postal service and the telegraph, the newspaper industry had become very capable at news gathering, being able to print and distribute papers containing reports on the previous day's events. They had also perfected the technique of news copy-writing, with a great density of facts often contained in one or two succinct sentences that were still easy to read.

The recent digitisation of hundreds of local and regional newspapers has made finding and assembling these stories much more convenient than manually searching a limited number of titles at local archives. This is the main reason for the distant origins of some of the sources quoted in this compendium.

The vast majority of news concerns the direct actions of people, and the conditions under which the majority of the populace lived and worked in the era under consideration were very different from those pertaining today. Housing, health-care and working conditions for example, are all immeasurably better today. Nevertheless, we shouldn't get carried away with the idea that people were themselves somehow different. They felt the same emotions and had the same motives as people before and since although conventions may have allowed or compelled them to act in ways that wouldn't be seen as 'normal' or sensible today.

It is almost impossible to consider the four 'W' towns covered by this book without looking at those places in-between because they are so intimately linked, especially Bilston, Darlaston, Hill Top and to a lesser extent Tipton and Great Bridge. A small number of stories also relate to other areas a few miles outside of the towns themselves but hopefully they will still be of interest. I have generally given only a brief account or even omitted stories that are well known and have been told many times before.

Some stories are chosen not because they are especially important or even newsworthy but because they give a glimpse into conditions and attitudes of the era. I have included names, dates and streets because these can be very useful to social and family historians who might want to look deeper into particular stories and nothing brings history home like knowing it happened in your back yard! The lists of surnames and street names at the end of the book should also be of help in this regard.

While many newspaper reports can be shown to contain errors, these are most often in the fine detail such as spelling of names, ages, addresses and so forth - the general gist of the story is almost always correct. Where possible I have cross-checked with censuses, registries, directories and so forth but as it is almost impossible to check some of the details, I may have unwittingly repeated errors in the original articles.

Paul Robinson, Coven, Staffordshire, 2013

"Wise men say, and not without reason, that whoever wishes to foresee the future must consult the past; for human events ever resemble those of preceding times. This arises from the fact that they are produced by men who have been, and ever will be, animated by the same passions and thus they must necessarily have the same results." Machiavelli

Explosions, Fire and Pestilence

Chapter 1

Explosions at collieries, railways and in industry were all too common in the nineteenth century until stricter regulation and inspection, and better technology came into being in the mines, factories and railway locomotives that were so prolific throughout the Black Country. The devastation and loss of life were sometimes spectacular and, of course, always tragic for the families of those concerned.

These days, precautions against fire are meticulously enshrined in law but despite being universally feared, people and organisations in days gone by often carried on in ways that are almost unthinkable today. Add to this the rudimentary fire-fighting forces and equipment available and it is understandable that often the best that could be hoped for, was that an outbreak could be contained and that there was no loss of life.

Wednesbury, Moxley and Darlaston were plagued by underground fires throughout the century due to the closeness of the coal seam to the surface and the sheer amount of human activity which provided ample opportunity for ignition. Photographs showing these can be found on old postcards and the phenomenon is reflected in local names such as 'The Fiery Holes'.

The industrial towns of South Staffordshire also had their fair share of pestilence in the nineteenth century with recurrent outbreaks of smallpox, cholera, typhoid and more. While these diseases could occur anywhere, their frequency and rate of contagion were greatly increased by the squalid conditions to be found in large parts of the boroughs.

Distillery Destroyed

In December 1842, a serious fire broke out at the works of John Bethell and Co, gas-distillers of West Bromwich. As might be expected, the fire was extremely fierce and consumed some 7,000 gallons of creosote, about 2,000 gallons of tar and the entire offices of the firm. It must have created quite a smell and pall of smoke across the town. According to the report, there was no insurance cover although the business must have survived, as it was later acquired in part by Robinson brothers.

Yorkshire Gazette 31st December 1842
Sandwell Community History and Archives Service

Repeat Performance

At around 3am on 7th January 1852, one of three boilers at Davies & Bloomer's ironworks at Golds Hill exploded with great violence, the noise being heard throughout the neighbouring towns of Wednesbury, Dudley and West Bromwich.

The boiler, which was designed to operate at a pressure of 40 pounds per square inch, had been carefully constructed from half-inch thick plate. In fact, extra care had been taken in it's manufacture as it was a replacement for a boiler that had exploded just five years beforehand!

The man who looked after the works steam engine, one Daniel Bradbury, had an extremely lucky escape. When it became necessary to stop the engine, a bell would sound to alert Bradbury if he was elsewhere in the works. In this instance he was beside the boiler in question with three other men when the bell rang. As he made his way to the engine the boiler erupted; Bradbury escaped but the three other men were killed outright. A fourth man was also killed although there was no outward sign of injury on his body.

London Standard Thursday 8th January 1852

Evening Explosion

A boiler exploded at the Moxley Street ironworks in Wednesbury during the evening of 28th September 1868. The explosion destroyed part of the forge and the boiler itself was thrown fifty yards across the adjacent canal.

The blast happened just as the night shift had begun at around seven o'clock - it killed five men and seriously injured three others.

Manchester Courier and Lancashire General Advertiser 3rd October 1868

Smallpox At Walsall

There were several outbreaks of smallpox at Walsall from the late 1860's until the end of the century. This terrible disease, which caused severe blistering of the skin and on occasion deformity and blindness, had a one in three mortality rate.

In the summer of 1872, the epidemic at Walsall was described as severe and the town had the highest quarterly death rate in the country from this disease at over 45 deaths per thousand population. Dudley was the next worst affected with a rate of almost 39 per thousand.

In a typical week in July, smallpox accounted for one death at Rushall, one at Bloxwich and nine in Walsall itself. Since the start of the outbreak, the Workhouse had treated over one hundred cases, twenty four of which had proved fatal.

Vaccinations were being carried out at schools throughout the area and success rates were reported as good; the officer at Darlaston for example, reporting no new cases for over a week and no deaths from the disease for almost a month.

The 'epidemic hospital' was built at Deadman's Lane running between Stafford Street and Green Lane following the 1872 outbreak. To encourage those infected to attend, the road was sensibly renamed to Hospital Street!

There was a further serious outbreak in 1875, and in 1888 Walsall was once more in the grip of an epidemic. In one typical week in April, there were half a dozen cases reported in the Workhouse hospital and a similar number in the borough hospital. By June, one weekly report listed double that number at the Workhouse and twenty two patients in the hospital

Five years later contagion visited Walsall once more but with each epidemic, analysis of the source and spread of the disease became more rigorous.

This time the Medical Officer reported that the first confirmed case, in March, was in a tramp who had been lodging at New Street. He and his family were treated at the hospital and no more cases were reported until May when an unvaccinated child at Hollyhedge Lane presented a serious attack which could be directly traced back to Birmingham.

The Medical Officer said that the girl's friends and relatives had acted carelessly in visiting her and thereby spreading the infection throughout the Hollyhedge Lane area. In July, two severe cases came to light in Adam Street and these were in relatives of the young girl.

A separate source was brought to the town by a servant girl, again from Birmingham, who was working at a public house in Bridgeman Street. This caused a major epidemic of around 400 cases to spread to all outlying areas of the town and was exacerbated by people having evaded the vaccination for some years.

Birmingham Daily Post 6th August 1872
Birmingham Daily Post 13th July 1872
Tamworth Herald 14th April 1888
Tamworth Herald 16th June 1888
Birmingham Daily Post 9th November 1893

Hat Shop Destroyed

Richard Parton and his wife ran adjacent shops at 64 and 65 Union Street, Wednesbury, he being a fruiterer and she a milliner. In 1883 there was a serious fire in the millinery side of the business resulting in its complete destruction.

Mrs Parton and her two children were lucky to be rescued although they were in a semi-conscious state due to smoke inhalation. Some fifty people helped prevent the blaze spreading to adjoining properties.

Western Daily Press 14th June 1883
1881 census RG11 piece 2853 folio 111 page 29

Brickworks Explosion

Four people lost their lives in a boiler explosion at Barrows' brickworks at Great Bridge in May 1882. Amongst the fatalities was a young woman who was due to be married the very next day.

Manchester Evening News 15th May 1882

Fuel Fire

The Wolverhampton firm of William Evans and Son were iron braziers; that is they specialised in joining metal by the brazing process which is similar to welding or soldering. In those days a brazing torch was fuelled by 'spirits of tar' such as Naphtha and a business such as Evans' would require substantial quantities of this dangerous liquid.

On the night of the first Monday in November 1869, a horrible fire broke out at Evans' works resulting in death and injury to nine people. The fire was accidentally started by two young women who were looking for a missing plug from a tap. The first, Martha Williams, went to the stove room and lit a piece of paper to provide light by which to search the floor for the plug. On her way back she inadvertently dropped the paper which set fire to her paper apron(!) and the clothes of Maria Farren who came to help her douse the flames.

From this small act the brazing fuel was ignited and the resulting fire consumed the two storey workshop killing two women and a boy. As one of the women stood engulfed in flame the other leapt into the inferno to help and lost her life as a result. The boy had taken refuge inside an empty stove but died from the fumes of the fire. A fourth person later died of their injuries.

Williams and Farren survived to tell the grisly tale to the inquest jury but they were not found to be responsible - a verdict of accidental death was returned and businesses were implored to take care to store such fuel in a safe place!

Luton Times and Advertiser 6th November 1869
Manchester Times 27th November 1869

Birchill Hall Ironworks Disaster

Probably the most notorious accident of this kind occurred at the Birchill Hall works near Walsall in May 1880.

A 30 ton 'egg-ended' vertical boiler measuring some 30 by 8 feet exploded at about 10.30 on a Saturday morning killing thirty men and injuring sixty more.

The only warning of the impending explosion was a few seconds of 'heaving and swaying' before the boiler exploded in the most violent manner imaginable. It was thrust a great distance into the air before splitting into two main pieces. The escaping steam and the force of the explosion sent brickwork, parts of the furnaces and copious amounts of molten metal flying in all directions. One can hardly imagine the pitiful scene left behind and the effect that this must have had on the survivors, the many men and women who came to help and the families of the deceased and injured.

Sheffield Daily Telegraph 17th May 1880

Pedestrians Beware

An underground leak filled three cellars in Great Brick-Kiln Street, Wolverhampton with gas on the night of 10th November 1900. The subsequent explosion blew up thirty yards of pavement, destroyed newly laid electricity cable beneath and set fire to the adjacent houses. Fortunately there were no reports of injury.

Western Mail 12th November 1900

Morning Blast

On the 1st May 1882 there was an explosion at the Hall End Colliery in West Bromwich at the very start of the morning shift. One man, Albert Walker was detained at hospital for treatment of his burns and several others were treated as out-patients.

Birmingham Daily Post 2nd May 1882

Cellar Full Of Gas

The quiet of Sunday evening at Larches Lane, between the Tettenhall and Compton Roads in Wolverhampton, was shattered by a gas explosion in August 1862. The recently laid gas main running near to Phillip Bowater's house had sunk, causing gas to leak into a nearby drain which was in turn connected to his cellar.

From the cellar, gas seeped up the outside wall of the house and when Mr Bowater went into his parlour with a lighted candle an explosion ensued blowing out the glass from his window and setting fire to the frame. A more serious fire was averted by forcing the burning frame out from the wall and dousing it with water.

Birmingham Daily Post 14th August 1862
1861 census RG09 piece 1990 folio 65 page 18

Explosion At Swan Colliery

An explosion at the Swan Colliery, West Bromwich cost 28 year old 'cogger' Richard Hughes his life. Hughes was recovering timber from underground waste when the explosion occurred. It is believed that a roof fall had released gas into the mine which was ignited by the man's light.

Birmingham Daily Post 12th June 1878

Two Stones Of Powder

On 3rd November 1886 there was an explosion in the powder magazine at Burrow's Colliery on the West Bromwich Road in Wednesbury which resulted in one fatality and several injuries.

The person who died was fifteen year old Samuel Hawkins, the son of the chartermaster, who had just doled out a can of gunpowder to a miner named Thomas Eagles. When Eagles had walked around a dozen yards away a fearful explosion took place, igniting his can of powder which caused serious burns to himself and others who were in the path of the blast. Even those who were tens of yards away were knocked off their feet and the noise of the blast and the clouds of smoke it produced caused much alarm at the pit head. Needless to say, young Hawkins who was inside the powder store lost his life.

Around 28 lbs of powder were involved in the blast and two possible sources of ignition were isolated; a light by the powder store door, although that was always kept in the same place or, more likely, a spark caused by the young man's hob-nail boots. It is ironic that the event was first reported on Bonfire Night.

Birmingham Daily Post 5th November 1866

Black Lake Colliery Fire

A fire broke out at Horton and Sons colliery at Black Lake, West Bromwich during the night of 22nd November 1870 as a result of which seven men and a 12 year old boy lost their lives.

The inquest held the following January heard how the eight had eaten their supper whilst underground then lay down to sleep, leaving no-one to watch the mine. After considerable expert inspection, the fire was adjudged to have been started by a candle setting fire to a truss of hay suspended in the coal-hewn stable. Although a watchman was on the pit bank at the surface and the winding-engine was manned, the early stages of the fire remained undetected.

Aside from sleeping when they were supposed to be at work, the men had broken another safety rule by propping open a door to increase the temperature while they ate their supper but this had the fatal effect of shutting off the fresh air supply once the fire was burning.

Although one horse was consumed by the fire, the men died from the noxious fumes that spread above them as they slept. The inquest returned a verdict of accidental death and the mining agent, Mr Lawley, was exonerated.

Birmingham Daily Post 27th Jan 1871

Blazing Saddles

A fire was discovered on a Sunday evening in March 1895 at the premises of saddler, Mr F Willis, in Navigation Street. The railwayman who spotted the fire was on his way home when he saw the three storey building ablaze. He dashed round into Station Street to raise Mr Willis but the fire was too fierce for anything to be saved; the entire stock, materials and machinery were reduced to ashes leaving just the shell of the building. No cause for the fire could be determined.

Birmingham Daily Post 11th March 1895

Timber Yard Fire

A substantial fire broke out at Boys and Sons timber merchants in Walsall on 22nd May 1896 causing some £10,000 worth of losses. No cause for the conflagration could be determined but it destroyed much machinery and some 200,000 trenails (wooden pegs) destined for the railway companies. The fire was exacerbated by a preceding spell of dry weather and the creosote that was universally used to treat railway timber.

Sheffield Daily Telegraph 23rd May 1896

Burning Bedroom

In November 1889, the Central Fire Station at West Bromwich received word at one in the morning, that there was a fire at the Dartmouth Arms Inn on Sheepwash Lane, Great Bridge.

Captain Wayte and his crew were quickly on the scene and found that a bedroom was on fire. It was thought that a chimney fire in the kitchen had caused burning soot to fall into the bedroom fireplace, which was papered over. The paper had ignited and set fire to furnishings within the room, consuming almost the whole bed in which two children were sleeping. Miraculously both children escaped without injury.

Birmingham Daily Post 26th November 1889

Subterranean Fires

Wednesbury Town Council met on Saturday 15th February 1896 to discuss an underground fire at Old Park Road, where flames from burning coal beside and below the road lapped the considerable volume of traffic that passed over it! There was also the worry that once the coal was burned out the road would collapse.

The Kings Hill area was especially dangerous and people were prevented from wandering around the area by permanent police watchmen. In April 1897, a policeman who had gone to warn people to keep away from the place fell into a pit himself and lost his life. A number of officers searched for him but it was one courageous constable, Golby, who volunteered to descend into the deepest pit using a ladder to recover the man's body. The holes were said to be as bottomless as quicksand and filled with fine white ash. The flames, smoke and fumes were considerable and it took Golby two attempts before he bravely brought his deceased colleague to the surface.

At the end of April 1898 more fires were causing alarm in the centre of the town. Three fires were burning in Bridge Street and had caused damage to property including the collapse of walls.

Fires in the earth continued to affect roads and buildings in the area, for example at the Olympia Picture House in Bell Street, Darlaston, right up until the mid 20th century.

Sheffield Daily Telegraph 17th February 1896
Falkirk Herald 28th April 1897

Lichfield Mercury 2nd May 1898
National Archives D1230/BOX43/5

Works Destroyed

There was a serious fire at the nickel-plating works of Joseph Bates in Temple Street, Wolverhampton, in October 1884. The fire was discovered at 4am by a passing policeman but nothing could be done to prevent the destruction of the entire three-storey premises.

Birmingham Daily Post 15th October 1884

Butcher's Fish Shop Banger

Mr Butcher ran a fish shop in Paradise Street, West Bromwich in the 1890's. One evening when several people were in his shop there was an explosion of such severity that it blew out his shop window. Fortunately only one person, a barmaid from the nearby Albion Hotel, was slightly injured. An inspection found that a large gas-tap had been left open, allowing a considerable amount of gas to escape until the inevitable happened.

Birmingham Daily Post 9th September 1893

Cholera

In the filthy and overcrowded conditions that pertained in many parts of the Black Country in the nineteenth century, the threat of cholera was ever-present. This bacterial infection of the gut which was spread by consuming contaminated food or water, caused diarrhea and vomiting that could soon lead to dehydration and electrolyte imbalance. Given the poor diet and consequential fragile state of health of many people, death was always a distinct possibility for anyone unfortunate enough to contract the disease.

At West Bromwich in June 1866, three local clergymen petitioned the town Commissioners regarding the sanitary conditions in the town. At The Lyng, for example, open sewers were said to be clogged up with 'suds' and excrement from houses, and filth continuously piled up in the road at a spot where hundred of people passed each day. At Maria Street and Green

Street there were pools of green and stagnant water in the road and cholera was always present amongst the inhabitants. In the vicinity of St Peter's church at Greets Green, the gutters were stopped up and overflowing with offensive matter and at the rear of one property was a "dreadful pit of stagnant slime and filth". At Great Bridge the houses were generally in a very bad state and material removed when sewers were cleaned was simply left piled on the road surface.

At this same meeting the Commissioners received a letter from a waste contractor who was flabbergasted to hear that they thought one privy and ash pit between five or six houses was insufficient!

These conditions were by no means unique to West Bromwich. They were replicated (literally ad nauseum) in each of the towns with which we are concerned, and had been so for most of the preceding three decades.

Wolverhampton suffered its first two cases of cholera in 1832 at a lodging house in North Street. The victims, a young man and an old woman, had come from Bilston where the disease was already said to be raging violently. Within a few days there were twenty two cases and eight deaths in Wolverhampton and in August of that year the disease made its first appearance at Walsall. To begin with at least, the disease tended to affect those living in the most squalid conditions and was thought to be spread from place to place by vagrants.

At Bilston the disease had killed around five hundred people by the end of August, about three per cent of the population, including two surgeons. The strain on local industry increased as the workforce was depleted and business owners became ill, further increasing poverty and therefore the likelihood of contracting the disease. The coffin-makers there were said to be so busy that more coffins had to be ordered from Birmingham.

The 'wakes' at Bilston and Wednesbury, where huge numbers of people would gather and potentially cause calamitous spread of the disease were wisely suspended.

Aside from the initial outbreak in 1832 and that mentioned above in 1866, there were epidemics in the late 1840's and in the last two decades of the century. It was not until local bodies made significant progress in sanitary systems that the threat began to subside.

In the early days, one Liverpool surgeon put forward a cholera treatment which he claimed was most effective. The dose was three teaspoons of a concoction of Cayenne pepper in best French brandy repeated half-hourly if required. Exactly how the poor folk affected by the disease were supposed to come by such ingredients we can only wonder.

Staffordshire Advertiser 18th August 1832
Preston Chronicle 1st September 1832

Washed Away By Oil

Joseph Didcott died following a horrendous accident at the Robinson Brothers' chemical works near Greets Green, West Bromwich in 1876. He and two other men, Henry Dell and Caleb Bashford, were building an extension to the company's canal wharf when a large iron tank containing mineral oil suddenly burst open.

The large square tank held around 70 tons of oil which spewed out into the canal, demolishing a wall as it did so. Didcott was seriously injured by one of the fractured iron sheets from the tank and swept into the canal in a torrent of oil. Although he was rescued, his injuries were such that he died later the same day.

Bashford was also carried away by the oil but managed to extricate himself, while Dell managed to avoid the worst of it, although the force of the torrent broke his leg.

The tank had only been installed a few months beforehand and was supposedly built to withstand the weight of its contents. As boiling oil had been pumped into the tank the night before perhaps the tank could not cope with the pressure as well as the weight or maybe the men had disturbed the ground on which the tank stood causing it to fracture.

Edinburgh Evening News 5th May 1876

Boiler Explosion At Hall End

A terrible boiler explosion at Johnson's forge in Hall End, West Bromwich was widely reported over several weeks in 1864 and justifiably so as it was responsible for seven deaths and fourteen injuries.

Like the Birchills boiler, it was another of the vertical egg-shaped design that exploded. In this case one large fragment was blown forty yards up the road and landed on a canal bridge. Another was blasted high into the air and in falling, demolished a chimney stack that fell through the roof of the rolling mill where the men were at work.

Every building in the vicinity of the boiler was wrecked and the explosion sprayed molten metal and fire in all directions. The majority of the fatalities, four of whom were teenagers, were as a result of the falling structure.

Derbyshire Times and Chesterfield Herald 5th March 1864

Accidental Detonation

One Saturday in July 1885, two men were engaged in removing a large mass of iron from the surface at Jones' ironworks at Birchills, Walsall.

In addition to conventional tools, the men were also intending to use dynamite to break the mass apart. They had drilled a hole in the material and placed the charge when for reasons unknown, the dynamite suddenly exploded. The men were peppered with metal fragments one of which passed straight through the body of William Ayre and another "carried away his eyes". Despite this the poor man lived for another ten minutes. His colleague John Agers survived, although he was terribly injured.

A worker atop one of the 60 foot tall blast furnaces saw a heavy sledge-hammer that the men had been using blown 20 feet higher than his position.

Lichfield Mercury 17th July 1885

Playing With Fire

Ten year old George Gee of Bromford Lane, West Bromwich was brought before the Police Court charged with setting fire to a hay rick three days before Christmas 1882. Another boy, Thomas Parker, said he saw the lad playing with fire near the rick on the afternoon concerned.

Young Gee received a stern reprimand but was discharged as the Bench believed he had no malicious intent in starting the fire. The owner of the rick Charles Brookes, a horse dealer of Bull Street, found himself £20 out of pocket.

Birmingham Daily Post 2nd January 1883

Lamp Shop In Flames

Redman and Co. had two shops selling petroleum lamps and fuel in Wolverhampton in 1870, one at Snow Hill and another on Victoria Street. One April evening at about eight o'clock, a workman was repairing the engine that pumped fuel from the cellar to the shop when his blow-lamp set fire to some nearby paper.

The shop manager's wife, Mrs Williams, tried with the help of her sister to douse the flames but the fire caused the shop's lamps to burst. The fire spread rapidly to the shopfront with flames licking the first floor windows outside. The Fire Brigade were soon at the scene and rapidly brought the fire under control to the cheers of the large crowd that had gathered.

The shop was gutted and the first floor windows destroyed but the building was otherwise saved. It was thought that less than a gallon of fuel was consumed but the fire was of sufficient ferocity to scorch the doors of Mr Weaver's house on the opposite side of the road!

It was extremely fortunate that the reservoir of fuel in the cellar and a quantity of volatile benzoline that was stored at the back of the premises escaped the blaze.

Birmingham Daily Post 7th April 1870

Gunpowder In The Oven

A terraced house at Cobden Street off Steelhouse Lane, Wolverhampton was the scene of an explosion in November 1884. It was around midday on a Saturday that William Cole, a twenty six year old sheet metal worker and shooting enthusiast, was drying out about half a pound of damp gunpowder in an oven that the explosion took place.

Cole was a lodger at the house which was occupied by his uncle James Dyke and family. At the moment of detonation Cole was in the back yard but Mr Dyke's three year old daughter was playing in the room where the gunpowder was drying and she suffered serious burns to her face and chest.

The force of the blast was so great that furniture, parts of the oven and grate, the mantlepiece and bricks from the fireplace were scattered around the room. One of the doors in the room was blown off its hinges and windows on both floors of the house were broken. Mr Dyke's mother-in-law who was sitting by the back door suffered a minor injury to her leg from flying masonry.

The little girl, Sarah Dyke, was reported as progressing favourably in hospital and indeed she can be seen with her family living at nearby Gordon Street on the census taken seven years later.

Lichfield Mercury 21st November 1884
1891 census RG12 piece 2236 folio 55 page 29

Wednesbury Oak Explosion

An inquest was held at Tipton into the death of Simeon Didlock, a miner at the Wednesbury Oak colliery. Didlock was loading a hole with three pounds of gunpowder while using an unguarded candle and the almost inevitable explosion burned him to death. The inquest decided that it was an accidental death and that he was solely to blame.

Tamworth Herald 19th June 1880

The Fever Hole

Although less feared than cholera, typhoid fever was always a worry to the authorities, especially as there was no available vaccine until the very end of the century. The disease was transmitted in water contaminated with the faeces of those already infected and, given the poor drainage and filthy conditions in some areas, it was likely to emerge at any time.

A pool was made at Camp Street, Wednesbury in 1825 to store water for use in the huge condensing beam engine at the ironworks of George and William Lees Adams. The pool received drainage from High Bullen and Market Place until the late 1850's and after that it continued to be supplied by rainwater from the roofs of properties, a natural spring in the cellar of an adjacent house and by the South Staffordshire Waterworks' reservoirs. The pool was estimated to contain around half a million gallons in total and Messrs Adams were contracted to take 200,000 gallons from the Waterworks reservoirs each year.

The pool had been considered a serious risk to health by local doctors for many years and the area around the pool was known as 'The Fever Hole'. In 1866 the matter was brought before the court where Adams were charged with allowing a pool to exist on their premises which was so foul as to cause a nuisance and be injurious to the health of the neighbourhood

Evidence was taken over almost eight hours from experts, local residents and those with a vested interest in the pool. Medical evidence showed the incidence of typhoid to be 1 in 14 in the vicinity of the pool compared to about 1 in 90 in the town as a whole and a list of streets was produced which showed that none had escaped the disease during the previous year.

Mr Proctor, surgeon and medical officer to the Board, said that he had inspected the pool on numerous occasions and that although much lime had been thrown in, it still contained a large quantity of organic matter that at times emitted an exceedingly obnoxious stench, so much so that people in the neighbourhood could not leave their doors open. The water was, he said, as "green as a leek", a source of the most formidable class of diseases and the cause of many fatalities in the surrounding population.

Various witnesses said that the houses around were very damp and that a large number of pigs were kept in the area, although the pool was presently in a better state than it had been a year earlier. There was only surface drainage and as a result, water would frequently be exchanged between the pool and the street. The number and severity of typhoid cases were comparable to those at Fallings Heath where there was another large and fetid pool.

In short, all of the medical evidence indicated that removal of the pool would be hugely beneficial to the health of the district. In support of their reports, a local vicar had compiled statistics from the parish registers which revealed higher than average mortality rates in the streets around the pool.

The defence presented a number of witnesses including Mr Lloyd the Chairman of the Board of Health, who said the pool did not smell and that the medical evidence had been exaggerated. He also said that should the pool be removed, the cost of replacing the condensing engine at the works would probably drive the business elsewhere. In his opinion if the pool was cleaned out, properly lined with clay and walled off it would not present any health hazard.

Also for the defence, Dr Hill said he had examined a sample of the pool water and visited the site but could find nothing that was, in his opinion, injurious to health and an analytical chemist, Mr Bird, agreed. Joseph Russell of the Jolly Brewers Inn and four other local residents testified that they had never found the pool to be a nuisance.

At the end of the hearing the Stipendiary decided that the business would be allowed to keep the pool provided it made the improvements suggested by Mr Lloyd. George and William Adams however must have decided that the cost of making the improvements or replacing their engines was not viable as the works and all its machinery was put up for auction in the following November.

Birmingham Daily Post 27th September 1866
Birmingham Gazette 26th October 1867

Almighty Explosion

There had been a smell of gas in the church at Walsall for some time and after the service one Sunday night in October 1847, the beadle decided to find out where it was coming from.

As the congregation were still making their way out, he approached the churchwarden's pew, candle in hand, when there was an explosion that tore up the pews scattering timber in all directions. The poor man was killed on the spot but the remaining members of the congregation escaped injury.

Chelmsford Chronicle 15th October 1847

Fire And Theft

A fire broke out at a pawnbroker's shop in Rushall Street, Walsall at about eleven in the morning on Saturday 12th January 1839. The local fire engine was soon at the scene but it failed to make an impact on the furious blaze so a message was sent by express coach to Birmingham. An engine from the Birmingham Fire Office and another from the Norwich Union arrived very soon after and with the help of local volunteers, the fire was brought under control and extinguished by three o'clock.

One man who had been helping douse the fire, fell when the roof collapsed but escaped with minor injuries. Donations were given by many locals to help this man and to reward those others who took great risks to assist the fire crews.

As if the fire itself were not bad enough, it was accompanied by an influx of heartless thieves from as far away as Birmingham who descended on the place and carried off whatever remained of the stock! Mary Matthews, the owner of the shop, was insured for six hundred pounds but the final loss was calculated at five to six thousand.

As a corollary to the story, a more effective fire engine was sent from Birmingham to permanently protect the town and a number of the thieves were later apprehended.

Staffordshire Advertiser 19th January 1839

Clothing Fire

A twenty one year old man believed to be from the north of England was working at a brick yard in Walsall in 1841. The man, named Wood, had no regular lodgings but was sleeping rough in the area around the Windmill public house.

A little before midnight, one evening in late July, the publican, co-incidentally also named Wood, was tending to the fires around the inn. He shortly came upon upon the young man who at that instant jumped up crying "O lord! I am all on fire". The publican helped to extinguish the flames but the man was badly burned on his back and head. It was supposed that an ember had landed on his clothes while he was sleeping and set fire to his clothing.

The poor man lingered in hospital for eighteen weeks before finally succumbing to his burns and in all that time no-one came to visit or enquire after him.

Staffordshire Gazette and County Standard 23rd December 1841

Red Hot Cutting

While making a 30 foot deep cutting during construction of the South Staffordshire Railway near Wednesbury, workers encountered some old mine workings in a coal seam that ran to the surface. Despite the twin risks of subsidence and fire, the line was nevertheless laid such that the seam lay along its very centre.

In February 1850 the seam was reported burning, no doubt due to sparks from passing engines, and a team of navvies were engaged in putting out this "perfectly red hot" fire.

Bath Chronicle and Weekly Gazette 7th February 1850

Millfields Explosion

In May 1898 there was a gas explosion at the Millfields Colliery in Hateley Heath, West Bromwich in which seven miners suffered serious burns. The men were conveyed to the District Hospital - a distance of about three miles - in what must in those days have been an agonisingly slow journey. Sadly, two of the men succumbed to their injuries.

Coventry Evening Telegraph Thursday 25th May 1899

Firedamp At Pump House Colliery

The Pump House Colliery near Dudley Port was worked by father and son James and Thomas Bailey in 1835. The main shaft was over 200 yards deep and from the bottom of the shaft the works extended almost as many yards horizontally.

On Monday 9th November at about 5pm, there was an enormous underground explosion at the mine which shook the earth throughout the vicinity and was accompanied by a sound said to be equivalent to numerous cannon. Large amounts of coal were blasted high into the air from the mouth of the pit accompanied by dense smoke.

At the time of the explosion, about thirty men and boys were working the coal face at the extreme end of the horizontal shaft. Men in the neighbourhood including those from other works quickly converged on the pit and some bravely descended the shaft to search for possible survivors. One of the first to go down, a man known as "Walsall Will" lost his life - he was badly injured when brought up and was taken to a nearby hovel where he died. The accident also claimed three horses and another three were very badly burned.

Moses Buckstone and his son were working beside each other and miraculously survived the blast. At the inquest he emphasised that the men were issued with Davy Lamps and strict orders given to use them and said that the colliery was well ventilated. Buckstone had thrown himself to the ground when the explosion happened and lay there for five minutes. He then put on his shirt and waistcoat and with his son tried to escape but they were beaten back by sulphurous fumes. In the end they returned to where they had been working and waited until rescuers found them at nine o'clock. They were taken home but did not properly recover consciousness until 3am.

Buckstone believed that the source of ignition was a candle that had been placed on the ground to provide light by which the men could work. He had worked at the colliery for four years in which time there had been no accidents and in his opinion no blame should be attached to anyone for the fourteen lives that were lost.

Oxford Journal 14th November 1835

Accidents, Collapses and Freak Weather

Chapter 2

As the old adage says, what goes up, must come down, and this can apply to even the sturdiest structures if they have some unseen fault, or have been modified or overloaded. Likewise, there is a certain inevitability that any man-made object that moves will sooner or later find itself in contact with something unintended. Crashes, of course, involve the transport of the day and in the nineteenth century, horses, canal boats, steam engines and, in the later decades, trams were the options.

Whether travelling or not, we are always at the mercy of the weather and we can be just as readily caught out by a flood or gale today as could our ancestors, although our buildings are, in theory at least, better able to withstand such 'acts of God'.

Newspapers of the 1800's are littered with stories about people ascending in and leaping out of balloons, sometimes for research or in attempting a record, often in front of crowds of onlookers. Why so many chose to experiment in the vicinity of the mass of chimneys and dangerous industrial buildings in the Black Country one can only guess. Perhaps it was related to the number of spectators that could be drummed-up.

As the consequences of any accident in the 1800's could be much more serious than today, with many injuries virtually untreatable, it is surprising that people were often prepared to take the risks that they did.

Kiln Collapse

There are several reports of kilns collapsing during construction in Victorian times, especially the round type. For example, six men building a kiln on the Bilston Road in Wolverhampton, for contractor Herbert Holloway, were buried beneath a mountain of rubble when it collapsed. The men, who were all seriously injured, were taken to the General Hospital but whether or not they survived is not reported.

Nottingham Evening Post 9th March 1899

Fell From A Moving Tram

Elizabeth Jane Wilkes was returning to her home at High Street, West Bromwich on the eleven o'clock tram from Greets Green. She indicated to the conductor that she was at her stop but the vehicle didn't pull up and she alighted while it was still in motion. Not only did she stumble and fall to the ground, but one of the tram wheels ran over her left arm almost severing it. She was given first aid at the nearby Prince of Wales inn and thereafter taken to hospital where it was found necessary to amputate the damaged limb.

Birmingham Daily Gazette 5th July 1889

Girl In The Well

A young servant girl, employed by a Mr Lavender at Walsall, was washing down the yard one Saturday afternoon in February, when the cover protecting a disused well gave way and she fell 22 yards to the bottom. The well contained sixteen feet of water but, being closed up for so long and given the time of year, the water was very cold and the air damp. It was two hours before the girl was brought out but she had succumbed to hypothermia. An inquest found her death to be accidental.

Staffordshire Gazette and County Standard 18th February 1841

Theft Causes Two Deaths

John Salter, a labourer living at Beggars Row, Wednesbury was charged with theft of timber from a house in High Bullen but his actions had contributed to the death of two women and the injury of a third woman and a baby.

The house in question had been unoccupied for some months and although in reasonable condition originally, it had been constantly pilfered for timber and had become unstable. In September 1886 Salter and the three women, one carrying a baby, were involved in removing the main beam from the roof. They had got the beam to the ground and were sawing it up when a passing woman called to them that the chimney was shaking and about to fall but they foolishly laughed off her warning. Very soon after, an entire side of the building collapsed burying the four unfortunates in a mound of rubble.

The inquest gave a verdict of accidental death on the two victims, Costigan and Martin, and the case was initially heard in the Wednesbury Police Court. Despite the owner's wish not to press charges against Salter or the injured woman Alice Garnstone, the magistrate decided that the case should be heard at the county Quarter Sessions.

Huddersfield Chronicle 25th September 1886
Birmingham Daily Post 29th September 1886

Not A Safe Distance

An accident at the Monway Works of the Patent Shaft company in Wednesbury ended in the death of Henry Phipps, a 23 year old steam hammer operator, in October 1895. Alteration to the works involved the removal of two stacks and, since the first had been removed without incident, no-one anticipated a problem with the second. As a result, men working the steam hammer beside this second stack were allowed to carry on work as normal.

A bricklayer removed the top five or six courses of brickwork, then went to the manhole at the bottom and removed some bricks to inspect the steel lining. At this point the uppermost twelve feet of brickwork collapsed and fell onto the workers, all of whom escaped except Phipps who was buried under the rubble.

It transpired that the lining which should have be over a quarter of an inch thick was badly corroded and was little thicker than a piece of paper. The verdict at the inquest was 'accidental death' with no more than a rebuke to the company for not removing its workers to a safe distance before the demolition commenced.

Birmingham Daily Post 28th October 1895

Down The Plug-Hole

A shocking event occurred near the tunnel of the Birmingham Canal at Tipton in early 1865. The bottom of the canal, which passed directly over one of the Earl of Dudley's mines, suddenly collapsed and a huge volume of water rushed down into the chasm produced. A nearby boat loaded with pig iron was snapped in two, with one half being washed down the shaft. The canal was drained of water for a considerable distance putting it out of use for some time.

Birmingham Daily Post 17th January 1865

Roof Down

With a large site and many employees involved in heavy industry, it is inevitable that the Patent Shaft works at Wednesbury had its fair share of industrial accidents over the decades. As well as the collapse detailed above, another unusual accident happened when the roof of the new 'Basic Steel Works' at the site collapsed in early 1888, killing one man and injuring two more.

Nottingham Evening Post 1st February 1888

Fallen Audience

A lecture at the United Methodist Free Church in Ridding Lane, Wednesbury was attended by almost 1,000 people, around 300 of whom were standing on a temporary wooden gallery above the rest.

The supporting posts of the gallery were not laid on planks to distribute the weight, but stood directly on the inch-thick floorboards. As more people crowded onto the gallery, one or more of these supports were gradually driven through floor, rendering the entire structure unstable. Incredibly, an attempt to add more supports was made without removing any of the spectators!

Inevitably, within a short time the gallery collapsed, its load and the heavy structure falling on those below. The resulting injury and confusion was accompanied by great panic, with people frantically crowding around the exit doors.

Surprisingly only a handful of people were seriously hurt, although many suffered minor injuries.

Illustrated Police News 4th May 1867

Floor Overloaded

In March 1841 a floor collapsed at Hemmingsley & Co, Littles Lane, Wolverhampton due to the weight of iron placed upon it. A fourteen year old, Peter McDermott, lost his life and several others were injured. The inquest returned a verdict of accidental death.

Staffordshire Gazette and County Standard 25th March 1841

Fell From Scaffolding

Thomas Kelly, a seventeen year old labourer, was working on some new buildings in Rutter Street, Walsall one Saturday afternoon. As he walked along the scaffold carrying a mortar board, he lost his footing and fell to the ground. The serious head injury he sustained was the cause of his death at the Cottage Hospital an hour later.

The inquest heard that the walkway was only three planks wide in places and was completely unfenced.

Lichfield Mercury 27th June 1884
Birmingham Daily Post 24th June 1884

Dudley Incline Runaway

The London and North Western and Great Western railway companies each had running rights over a section of railway line, known as the Dudley Incline, that began near Dudley Port station. A Great Western passenger service from Birmingham joined this line early one Saturday morning in November 1867. Ahead of this train was a LNWR coal train, with a locomotive at either end, that had come to a stand on the 1 in 60 slope.

The lead engine of the coal train took some wagons off the front to deposit in a siding. Unfortunately the engine crew had made a terrible miscalculation, as the weight of the remaining fully loaded wagons was far too much for the lower powered locomotive at the rear to withstand. As a result it took off down the hill, driven on by the weight behind and shortly met the passenger train in a head-on collision.

Fortunately there were only five passengers on the GWR train and despite the violence of the crash neither they nor the footplate crew were fatally injured.

Chester Chronicle 23rd November 1867

Houses Buried

In October 1861, two three-storey houses at Wisemore, Walsall were consumed by the earth and completely buried. The houses were occupied by the families of two clerks, William Robinson and John Jasper, who worked for John Brewer junior. Mr Brewer worked limestone pits in the area and the two houses were very close to one of the pit shafts.

On Saturday 19th October, Brewer had the nagging feeling that all was not right in the workings and on Sunday he made an examination of them, as a result of which he told the occupants of the houses that if they had any regard for their safety, they should vacate them immediately. Despite this it took him several hours to convince them of the danger and they didn't leave the two properties until eleven in the evening.

At about 3am the event that Brewer had anticipated took place; a considerable area of ground around the houses collapsed, the houses and their contents being completely swallowed up.

The dwellings were valued at about £450 each plus the furniture and possessions they contained.

As far back as 1828, a croft at Wisemore had been auctioned by Mr Brewer senior. In the auction particulars, limestone was said to be within a few fields of the property and was expected to continue underneath.

Manchester Times 26th October 1861
Birmingham Gazette 8th September 1828

Steam Tram Smash

Although steam trams were on the streets for a relatively short time, and like any tram were not free to wander off course, they nevertheless had their fair share of accidents. Letters to newspapers of the day show that steam trams had many detractors because of the smoke and noise they emitted, but they were a boon to workers, who could get a ride home for a penny after a long day at work, rather than walking.

A typical steam tram accident happened at Dudley Street, Wednesbury in August 1900 when an engine and its tram car collided with a vehicle driven by one William Parker of West Bromwich. Parker's vehicle (presumably a cart of some sort) was apparently "broken into matchwood" and he suffered critical injuries.

Thomas Rushton was driving a horse and trap belonging to Mr Benton, a Dudley Street grocer, when it collided with a steam tram at Snow Hill, Wolverhampton. The horse and cart were turned over but no-one was injured.

In 1887, the wife and two daughters of Wolverhampton brewer Mr Hodson, were riding out in a phaeton (a lightweight, pony-drawn carriage), when an approaching steam tram caused the pony to take flight.

The ladies were thrown from their vehicle and Mrs Hodson suffered a broken leg.

Sheffield Daily Telegraph 13th August 1900
Birmingham Daily Post 27th May 1889
Manchester Evening News 7th April 1887

Run Down At Ryecroft

Mr A C Cozens, a Wolverhampton ironmonger, had been to Walsall to visit friends and conduct some business. On his way home at night he attempted to cross the railway near the busy Ryecroft Junction, Walsall. He was run down by a train and his mangled remains found by a platelayer the next morning.

Bucks Herald 18th February 1888

High Level Collision

Two trains converged on Bushbury Junction on Saturday 2nd September 1865 at around 10pm, one a local service from Walsall, the other an express from Liverpool. Both were running late but the Walsall train was held back to let the express pass and it duly pulled in to the LNWR's High Level station.

While tickets were being collected, the Walsall train ran into the rear of the now stationary express with considerable force. Fortunately the Liverpool train had a substantial horse-box coupled behind the brake van, which absorbed much of the impact. Nevertheless, many passengers were injured, some seriously.

The driver of the Walsall train, Edward Jarvis, claimed that he had instructed his fireman to apply the brakes when he saw the signal against him but said that the fireman had instead reversed the brakes. For his part the fireman claimed that he had applied the brakes properly but that Jarvis was simply travelling too fast to stop in time.

In typical Victorian style, the line was cleared and the train, less a few damaged carriages and the injured passengers, was on its way within the hour!

Birmingham Daily Post 4th September 1865

Triple Tragedy

Near the end of December 1881, a rock-fall at the Park Hill Colliery near Walsall completely buried two men. When they were extricated, Joseph Lockley was dead and Patrick Bargen had a broken back. Mr Bargen's six children also had no mother as just three weeks before the colliery accident she had lost her way in the fog and was drowned.

Staffordshire Sentinel 30th December 1881

Wednesbury Hurricane

Tremendous winds struck the West Midlands on Wednesday 13th January 1886, causing buildings to be unroofed and greenhouses to be destroyed at Wolverhampton. At Wednesbury the winds toppled a 20 ton steam crane at the Patent Shaft works, killing it's driver William Darlington. The entire engine from a second crane was blown off and destroyed.

Sheffield Independent 14th January 1886

Swingboat Accident

Fourteen year old Charles Henry Lycett of Reedswood, Walsall went to the circus with a friend on the evening of Tuesday 11th June 1889, and later, at around half past ten, he went to some swing-boats that had been set up on adjacent land.

He was offered a seat in a stationary boat by the lad in charge but wanted to get into one that was already moving. The young attendant warned Charles not to try to get into the moving boat but he paid no heed and jumped towards it, with the intention of bringing it to a halt. Unfortunately he mis-timed his leap and the boat hit him full in the face, knocking him backwards into the gutter. When picked up he was unconscious and bleeding from the nose and mouth. He was conveyed to hospital but passed away less than twenty four hours later.

The inquest jury's verdict was accidental death but they also requested that the coroner write to the local Corporation asking for a regulation to be introduced that would compel any such amusement to be fenced-in and the entrance managed.

Birmingham Daily Post 14th June 1889

Widespread Wind Damage

Wild winds tore across the region for two days, almost exactly five years before the Wednesbury Hurricane, causing numerous calamities.

At the Castle Ironworks at Birchills, Walsall, George Meredith and George Lake were descending the incline from the furnace top with an empty wagon when the men and their vehicle were blown clean off the slope by a tremendous gust of wind. Meredith was killed instantly whereas Lake suffered a severed leg and fractured skull but died while being carried to the Cottage Hospital.

In Coseley, Princess End and Woodsetton there were fallen chimneys, ripped off roofs and fallen walls. In Wednesbury a stone cross was blown off the spire of St John's church; it fell through the church roof and destroyed a pew.

There were injuries reported at Tipton, and two old houses at Dudley Port were partially destroyed with the occupants slightly injured. At Monmore Green part of a works was blown down and in Wolverhampton the gable end of the Shamrock Inn was not so lucky when it crumbled into the street!

Worcester Journal 22nd January 1881

Walsall Under Water

In mid-1875 the River Tame at Walsall rose so high that it overflowed and filled the station up to the level of the platform. At the same time the town's Arboretum lake rose substantially and flooded the surrounding area.

Sheffield Daily Telegraph 22nd July 1875

Lightning Strikes Two

In the peak season for such events, lightning hit a house at Wolverhampton in June 1879. The bolt passed down the chimney breast and struck the householder, Mrs Morrison, and a three year old neighbour, Sarah Ann New. The little girl didn't regain consciousness and died two days later of her burns. Mrs Morrison was reported as still confined to bed a week after the event.

Manchester Evening News 17th June 1879

Death In The Cutting

Caleb Harvey, a labourer for the Walsall and Wolverhampton Railway who lived at Dudley, was working on an embankment in the cutting near the Birchills Farms, Walsall in May 1871. Somehow he managed to fall between a train of ballast wagons, three of which passed over him, completely mangling his body.

Birmingham Gazette 20th May 1871

Chimneys Hit

In midsummer 1865 the tallest stack at Sparrow's iron works at Horseley Fields, Wolverhampton was struck by lightning and about thirty bricks were dislodged. These were hurled some distance and fell through the roof of a forge where men were working, although none were injured.

At Wednesfield Heath the chimney stack at the house of LNWR goods manager Mr Huntley was partially destroyed and similar but more serious damage was done at the nearby beer house run by a Mr Cope.

Leeds Mercury 11th July 1865

Low Level Lunacy

On Wednesday 12th August 1896 Samuel Greenfield, a resident of Dudley, was a little late for his train from Wolverhampton Low Level station to Birmingham. Rather than use the footbridge he decided to head straight for the 'up' platform from the level crossing.

He was grabbed on two separate occasions by railway employees who recognised the peril Greenfield was putting himself in but despite this, he struggled and broke free on each occasion only to be finally run down by the train. He was badly cut and bruised but his main injury was an almost totally severed left arm which was amputated when he arrived at the General Hospital. Despite the loss of an arm, both he and Hobbins, one of the railway workers who was almost dragged under the train while trying to apprehend him, were lucky to escape with their lives.

Lichfield Mercury 14th August 1896

Severely Scalded

In August 1862, Henry Farmer a locomotive fireman, was seriously injured at the GWR's Stafford Road works in Wolverhampton. For some inexplicable reason, rather than tightening a wash-out plug on his engine he unscrewed it, releasing a blast of high-pressure steam from the full boiler.

Birmingham Daily Post 14th August 1862

Tram Trap

As noted elsewhere, tram lines could prove a serious hazard to pedestrians, cyclists and other vehicles. In October 1884 licensed victualler Mr Onions and his two children were badly shaken after being thrown from their horse drawn trap. The wheels of their vehicle had fouled the tracks at Five Ways, Wolverhampton.

Birmingham Daily Post 15th October 1884

To Jump Or Not To Jump?

In mid-1889 a young man by the name of Walter Mizen made arrangements to parachute from a balloon over Wednesbury. In the event, the balloon was unable to gain sufficient height to make a safe jump but was instead carried horizontally, at an altitude of around 200 feet, towards West Bromwich.

Eventually Mizen decided that jumping was a better bet than staying with the balloon and when over West Bromwich, he decided to take his chance. He deployed his parachute immediately but it didn't have time to fully open before he landed on the roof of a building. He was taken to hospital with concussion and facial injuries.

Hull Daily Mail 30th July 1889

Performance Cut Short

The wooden gallery of a temporary theatre at West Bromwich collapsed five minutes after a performance had begun but despite the screams of men, women and children who were pitched onto the benches below, only one woman appeared to be slightly injured.

However, when the fallen structure was removed, the body of twenty four year old Benjamin Rubery was discovered. He was in a kneeling position with his hands on the floor and his head forced down between his shoulders.

The inquest, which was held at the Hare and Hounds, Mayers Green, came to the conclusion that the young man had sneaked under the stage to avoid paying for entry and, in forcing his way through some woodwork to get a view of the performance, had dislodged the gallery supports. The jury found that there was no negligence on the part of the proprietor and issued a verdict of accidental death.

Fife Herald (from the Birmingham Journal) 2nd September 1845

Falling Like Kitty

When it came to leaping out of balloons, women could be as brave (or reckless) as men but 'Kitty King' didn't get the opportunity to prove this, at least when she attempted it at the recreation grounds at Hill Top, West Bromwich in 1899.

The balloon had only risen to around 12 feet above the ground when one of the ropes broke or came undone and Miss King was unceremoniously dumped on the ground. So far as is known, she suffered only a shock to the system and no doubt much injured pride.

The unfettered balloon took off on its own adventure and was found some time afterwards in a field near Old Church!

Manchester Evening News 4th April 1899

Cellarman Falls From Upstairs Window

John Hughes was a nineteen year old cellarman who worked at the Walsall Railway Station refreshment rooms. One Friday afternoon in September 1890, he was cleaning a window in a second storey room when he lost his footing and crashed through a glass roof onto Platform 1. He was taken to hospital with a fractured skull.

Birmingham Daily Post 27th September 1890

Chimney Magnet

A failed balloon ascent happened at Willenhall at the end of August 1888. The pilot was a man named Lemperi and he was accompanied by a local surgeon, Dr Tonks.

A collision with a workshop chimney deposited brickwork in the 'car', preventing it from rising further, and it consequently crashed into the chimney of a house before the silk envelope was finally torn from top to bottom, putting an end to the misery. The men got away with light injuries, the worst being an injury to the surgeons leg caused by the grapnel.

Aberdeen Evening Express 30th August 1888

Windy Walsall

In the winter of 1877, two roofs were completely blown off houses in Church Street, Walsall and a caravan at the showground was blown onto its side.

Birmingham Daily Gazette 31st January 1877

Killed On The Crossing

An inquest was held at Birmingham in October 1864 into the death of John Tanday of Hill Top, West Bromwich. Sixty one year old Mr Tanday made and sold ginger beer, especially to three of the larger ironworks at Wednesbury: Solly's, Barker's and Bagnall's. On a Saturday afternoon, he had gone to collect money that was owed to him from the three works and his route took him over the level crossing at Golds Hill.

The signalman at the crossing, Joseph Preston, said that when the Great Bridge to Wednesbury train approached at half past six, he checked that the line was clear and signalled the train to continue. After it had passed, and as was his habit, he to went to see that everything was in order with the crossing gates. While checking the gates, he noticed a basket lying on the 'down' line on the Wednesbury side of the crossing and, three or four yards beyond that, a figure between the rails.

Tanday had suffered a fractured arm, shoulder and ribs, and compound fractures to both legs. He died as a result of shock and loss of blood. Although direct evidence was almost non-existent, it seemed certain that he had been run over by the train and a verdict of accidental death was returned.

Birmingham Gazette 15th October 1864

Flower Fete Fiasco

Wolverhampton Corporation arranged for a Mr Spencer to provide tethered balloon flights at the annual flower show held in the town park in 1896.

Just as the first ride was about to begin, the gas-filled balloon broke away from the steel hawser that tethered it, rose rapidly into the sky and burst at around 500 feet. Fortunately no-one had managed to board the vessel before it decided to take its leave!

Grantham Journal 11th July 1896

Changed His Mind

A journalist and a hotel proprietor accompanied well-known 'aeronaut' Mr Whelan, on his ill-fated balloon flight from Horseley Heath, Wolverhampton in August 1891.

As is sometimes the case, the balloon did not rise satisfactorily to begin with, so the journalist jumped out at low altitude. Relieved of a third of its ballast, the balloon now shot up into the air. Whether the stress of the ascent had damaged the balloon or there was some other mishap is unknown, but shortly after its vigorous climb the balloon made an equally rapid descent, crashing through several house chimneys and badly injuring Whelan and the hotelier as it did so.

Gloucester Citizen 26th August 1891

Flying Footwear Renders Boy Speechless

In the course of a domestic dispute, Joseph Turner, a metal caster who lived on High Street, Wednesbury, threw a boot at his wife. The boot missed its intended target and instead struck a boy named John James on the head, making an indentation in his skull. The blow caused the boy to lose his speech entirely and he was admitted to West Bromwich hospital as a result.

Birmingham Daily Post 15th October 1884

Killed While Making Tea

A labourer named Timmins, who lived in a row of houses near Old Church, West Bromwich was struck and killed by lightning while filling a teapot. The strike made a hole in the roof of his house, burned the curtains and bedding in an upstairs room then emerged downstairs and struck him on the back of the neck. A small black mark on his skin was matched to a hole in the collar of his shirt and his daughter said that she saw fire at the back of his neck when he was struck.

Birmingham Journal 7th September 1867

Lucky Escapes

William Smith's house near the church at Heath Town, Wolverhampton was damaged inside and out by lightning in September 1867, although he did not witness the event. It tore through his roof, cracked ceiling plaster, broke a pane of glass and set fire to a trunk of clothing before it reached the ground floor.

In the downstairs sitting room, it stripped the plaster from one wall, burnt the paper on another and scattered pot plants around the room! There was more damage outside - the garden gate latch and hinges were fused, part of the gate was splintered and a nearby brass tap melted. A young man who was in the yard at the time miraculously escaped injury.

Mrs Smith and her grown-up daughter, who were downstairs, found all the rooms filled with smoke. Two children had been sleeping in the room where the trunk was ablaze, and the two ladies now dashed upstairs to discover their fate. Fortunately neither was injured although one was 'stupefied' for some time after the event.

Birmingham Journal 7th September 1867

Slip Up

Robert Harrison worked as a porter for Mr Harvey a grocer of Lichfield Street, Walsall. At about eight o'clock one winter's evening he walked up Paddock Lane, carrying a tub of butter weighing over three stones on his head. He slipped on the snow and fractured his leg.

Birmingham Daily Gazette 30th January 1865

Fell Into Molten Iron

Richard Grigg, a thirty two year old metal worker at the Crookhay works in West Bromwich, suffered a dreadful accident at work. His job was to run off molten iron from the furnace but on this occasion, finding too much material for the casting vessel at hand, he hastened to divert it into another. In his haste, he tripped over a piece of iron and fell headlong into the red-hot liquid. His face, chest and one arm were very badly burned and he was conveyed to the hospital at Birmingham for treatment.

London Daily News 12th February 1846

Captain Dight, Major Embarrassment

This well known inventor and aeronaut suffered scratches, bruises and probably dented pride when his balloon would not ascend at Wolverhampton. He was dragged through some trees then dashed to the ground on the racecourse, his balloon torn and apparatus damaged.

Shields Daily Gazette 20th April 1875

Saved By His Shoe

An accident at Hateley Heath colliery in 1841 cost three men their lives but one man had a miraculous escape from near certain death.

The three men who died were laying bricks near the bottom of a shaft when a bowke (a large metal bucket) full of bricks, fell into it. The bodies of Thomas Ward, Thomas Gibbons and Richard Knight were terribly mangled by the weight of the falling mass.

John Holden had just emerged from a pit when the accident happened and he saw the bowke, followed by banksman James Lewis, falling into the shaft. He ran to the edge of the shaft and found Lewis dangling there suspended only by his shoe which had caught on something at the lip of the hole!

The cause of the accident was attributed to the fact that there were no stop-blocks on the rails that reached almost to the edge of the shaft where the bowke was loaded.

Up until 1846 when the concept was abolished in English Law, any article that could be proven to have caused a death was forfeited to the crown. This 'deodand' could then be disposed of and any income given to some charitable cause. In this case a deodand of 10 shillings was levied on the bowke.

Staffordshire Gazette and County Standard 29th July 1841

Run Over In Wednesbury

A deodand of one shilling each was put on the wheels of a stagecoach belonging to George Bayley of Darlaston. Although travelling very slowly through Wednesbury, he ran over four year old Mary Ann Lucas. The child died at the scene but no blame was attributed to Bayley at the inquest in 1839, where "accidental death" was the finding.

Staffordshire Advertiser 14th September 1839

Drowned At The Swimming Pool

Fifteen year old Samuel Cheadle of Lower Stafford Street drowned at the Corporation Baths in Wolverhampton in the summer of 1883. As he was a competent swimmer, no-one was held responsible and the coroner was of the opinion that he had suffered cramp or a seizure. The jury gave a verdict of "death from accidental drowning".

Birmingham Daily Post 15th August 1883

Accident At The Sawmill

The firm of Couse and Bailey ran a sawmill at Paradise Street, West Bromwich and one of their customers was Henry Simms, a coal dealer of nearby Scotland Passage. Simms also sold sawdust, which he obtained from this sawmill, and his thirteen year old son Alfred, often went there on his behalf to bag-up the material.

One day in August 1889, John Roberts, an employee at the mill heard one of the leather bands used to drive machinery beating on the floor in a room below. This was usually an indicator that the band had snapped and would require mending. When he went down to investigate he was met with a shocking sight; the mutilated body of young Simms lay beneath one of the pulleys.

It seems that Alfred had taken it upon himself to use a grindstone in this room to sharpen a knife. He had dragged the grindstone stand some six feet towards to the pulley and spliced an unused belt to drive the machine. Somehow he had become entangled in the mechanism and as a result met his death. The blood-stained knife that he was trying to sharpen was found over twenty feet away.

At the inquest which was attended by Her Majesty's inspector of factories Captain Bevan, Mr Chatwin the works manager said that young Simms had no right to be in the room. Witnesses James Hunt and Enoch Bradley gave evidence that the area was fenced off and that the boy would have had to get over or under the fence to access the machinery.

The jury decided that death was accidental but recommended that fencing around the machinery be improved to prevent any such tragedy happening again.

Birmingham Daily Post 26th August 1889

Shunting Horse Accident

Despite their great ability for moving around large quantities of goods and people, the railways still relied on horses at stations and goods yards to get passengers and cargo to their final destinations and to shunt wagons. Robert Howard, a thirty year old carter, was running along in front of an empty wagon that was being moved along a siding by a horse. For some unknown reason the usually well-behaved animal suddenly took fright and ran around the wagon towards the rear. The chain by which it was attached caught Howard around the chest and squeezed him against the buffers, severing a finger and breaking his ribs which led to his death the following day. Coincidentally Howard lived at Railway Street, Horseley Fields.

Birmingham Daily Post 10th June 1893

Town Centre Burst

At about 6am on Tuesday 9th August 1859, part of the embankment near the wharves in Walsall town gave way, and a considerable amount of water was released. The adjacent streets were deluged, with some of the nearer houses flooded to a depth of a yard and a half. The landslip was directly attributable to old mine workings in the area, which were also to provide relief from the flood - the earth filling one such shaft collapsed and allowed the majority of the standing water to drain away.

The canal was completely devoid of water for some distance but further loss was averted by closing lock gates and putting in place temporary dams.

Birmingham Gazette 15th August 1859

Going Up, Going Down

It seems it wasn't always necessary to be in or even near an airship to be injured, just watching from afar was apparently enough.

A launch from Bellevue Gardens in Rood End took place at around 7pm one July evening in 1885. About a dozen workers at the nearby Albright & Wilson works decided they would like to witness the event, so they used the works lift to obtain a good vantage point.

When the night-shift manager called them back to work the men all got into the lift at once and, as the brake was not designed to withstand such a heavy load, the cage plummeted 70 feet to ground level. Three of the men suffered broken legs and internal injuries which were treated at West Bromwich hospital. Whether or not they saw the balloon launch was not reported.

Lancaster Gazette 18th July 1885

Accident At Wednesbury Station

John Barratt of Lower Dudley Street, Wednesbury, was a thirty seven year old repairman in the employ of the London and North Western Railway. At the end of a days work, he and a colleague arrived by train at Wednesbury a little after 5.30pm and, after alighting, he crossed the line near the level crossing to pick up some letters from the station.

As the train pulled out, a porter, Henry Derry, heard a woman screaming and upon investigating found Barratt lying in the 'four foot' in a crumpled heap. His legs and one arm were almost completely severed from his body.

The poor man was carried to the porter's room and a surgeon hurriedly summoned. The most the doctor could do was to administer brandy and water; as soon as he arrived he said that the fellow would not survive as he was so badly injured. In a little while Barratt regained consciousness, saying to the porter "Harry, this is a bad job" and holding out his hand to shake the hands of those around him whom he recognised.

It was supposed that Barratt had been knocked down by a train being shunted through the station towards the Great Western yard. The train consisted of an engine, two wagons and a brake van which was running with the latter foremost. It seems that he was knocked down by the van and pushed along by the underside of the locomotive for about twenty yards until a hollow in the permanent way was reached, although no trace of blood could be found on any part of the train. Accidental death was the verdict returned by the inquest jury.

Birmingham Daily Post 31st December 1886

Recreation and Rip-Off

Chapter 3

A large proportion of men and women working in Black Country towns in the nineteenth century had exceptionally hard jobs. They worked long hours in poor and often dangerous conditions, in mines, iron works and factories and on the canals, roads and railways.

Beer was a primary means of recreation for many men and the problems that came with it can be found throughout this book. By today's standards there were a phenomenal number of public houses in every town, some were long established inns, whereas others were simple 'beer-houses' or 'beer-shops' and many were home to all sorts of activity other than drinking!

Shows, sports and contests of all kinds were as common as now, with large fairs and 'wakes' as popular as today's music festivals. Without the level of security found at major events today, the opportunities that these gatherings presented to unscrupulous characters must have been enormous.

Although dog and cock-fighting were outlawed in the 1830's, it was very difficult to control illicit contests as they could be arranged at short notice and held pretty much anywhere, as long as it was out of the earshot of others. No doubt some spectators enjoyed these bloody fights for their own sake but they were primarily held for gambling, thereby adding vice to barbarity.

Even in the simple pleasure of eating, whether out or at home, people did not always get what they bargained for in their meals. The adulteration of food in the nineteenth century was a serious problem, both in terms of fraud and the health risk it might present to the unwitting buyer. The more common frauds perpetrated by dishonest sellers included sawdust mixed in with tea, chicory substituted for coffee, margarine for butter, and anything that could be watered down or 'bulked up' frequently was.

Whatever form of recreation people sought, money was required to pay for it, and as long as there has been money, there have been people prepared to take the risk of counterfeiting. Although milled coins improved throughout the eighteenth and nineteenth centuries, making them harder to copy, it was still possible for those with the necessary skill to create fakes in a cheap base metal, with a plated surface. If sufficient could be made and passed off (or "uttered"), the gains were potentially enormous and so therefore, to some, was the temptation.

Solicitor Charged

Mr Sheldon, a solicitor of High Street, Wednesbury, also owned a dairy farm at Wood Green. A woman employed by Sheldon took the milk each day and sold it around town, but in March 1874 she had the misfortune to sell some to Samuel Toy, an assistant inspector appointed under the Adulteration of Food Act. Toy had the milk tested and it was found to be 9% water.

In court, Sheldon said that he and his family had witnessed the milk brought to their kitchen by the cowkeeper and taken away by the woman, with no watering-down having taken place. He concluded that the woman, who had been in his employ for fourteen years, had taken the milk home, siphoned some off and replaced it with water.

As the legal vendor of the milk, Sheldon was accountable – he was found guilty and fined £5 plus costs.

Tamworth Herald 18th April 1874

Trading Sub-Standard

At Wolverhampton Police Courts a number of traders were prosecuted and fined in early 1880:

- Mary Ruby, Bilston Street - £1 for selling milk that had been skimmed and watered down by 20%

- Catherine Fox, Little Brickkiln Street - £1 for selling skimmed milk

- William Lambert, Salop Street - £5 for selling 'butterine' as butter

In December 1882 local traders from the Tipton and Great Bridge area were fined for various types of adulteration:

- Thomas Dudley, Wood Street, Tipton - 40s for selling margarine as butter

- John Bates, New Road, Great Bridge - £1 1s 4d for milk containing 17% water

- Edward Jackson, Church Lane, Tipton - 10s for selling coffee with 95% chicory

- Thomas Marlow, Horseley Heath, - 5s for selling coffee with 53% chicory

- William George, Workhouse Lane, Tipton - 5s for selling coffee with 45% chicory

Similar cases were brought against a number of Walsall retailers in 1885:

- Job Woodall, Shenstone - £5 for milk adulterated with 17% water

- Thomas Goodwin, Bridgeman Street - £1 for milk adulterated with 17% water

- Henry Hughes, Holland & King Grocers, Walsall - £1 for coffee with 25% chicory

In most cases a term of imprisonment was an option and costs were applied. In any event, the damage to the reputation of the swindlers must have been far in excess of the fines imposed.

Birmingham Daily Post 14th January 1880
Birmingham Daily Post 20th December 1882
Tamworth Herald 5th December 1885

Running On Rails

In February 1846, a much-hyped two-man sprint over 160 yards took place at Four Ashes railway station, between Joseph Powell of Coven, alias 'the nigger', and Henry Book of Stafford known as 'the doctor'. Whether the race was run upon or beside the railway track is not recorded.

It was a typical winter's day with frost and light snow in the morning, but by three o'clock, the winter sun had broken through and the starter, using a method dating back to the days of Rome, dropped a handkerchief to signal the start.

Book pulled ahead at first but Powell, who was the slight favourite, powered on to win convincingly, much to the delight of his crowd of local supporters. The total money bet on the race was in excess of £100… which equates to around £5,000 today!

Yorkshire Gazette 21st February 1846

Doctor Vint

In 1891 Harry Moores, also known as 'Dr Vint', was charged with deception at Wolverhampton. He had been conducting 'mesmeric entertainments' in the town but they were revealed to be a sham, as he had installed a group of paid stooges amongst each audience.

Sheffield Evening Telegraph 24th November 1891

Professional Needle

"Atlas" performed feats of strength alongside his sister "Vulcana". During his act at the St. George's Theatre in Walsall, Atlas asked members of the audience to come up on stage and test the weights he was using for themselves, so they could see that his feats of strength were genuine. One person who took up this invitation was a rival strong man "Gatwick, the midget Hercules".

Gatwick, real name John Pedley, climbed onto the stage and began testing the weights. As he went to pick up the third one Atlas suddenly became very angry, and as Gatwick fearfully moved off toward the wings, Atlas dealt him a blow to the face in full view of the audience, blacking his eye and cutting his cheek. It was as a result of this assault that Gatwick looked to the courts for redress.

In court at the Guildhall, Atlas said that Gatwick had claimed that the act was a fraud on several occasions in the past, and that Gatwick's actions on the night in question provoked the attack. On stage, Atlas had offered £5 to anyone who could do with two hands what he could do with one, and when the diminutive Gatwick came up, he said he would give him £50 if he could do it.

Gatwick denied that he had said that Atlas's act was a fraud and also denied calling out that Atlas had been beaten by "Titan" at Sheffield!

Thomas Thomas, the show-master, said in evidence that the curtain was dropped as soon as the first blow was struck but that the pair had carried on fighting backstage despite his trying to separate them and receiving several blows himself in the process.

Gatwick said that unless he was booked to perform or compensated for his injury he would turn up at the show every night and cause upset.

In the end Atlas was fined ten shillings plus costs for the assault but whether Gatwick was satisfied with this outcome was not reported. "Atlas" refused give his real name in court and apparently there was no power to compel him to do so.

Worcester Journal 27th June 1896

Racing At Gailey

'Furious driving on the highway' isn't a charge that would feature in news reports today, but it did in the spring of 1891, even though the furious speed involved was only 17 miles per hour.

The case was brought against six men following a 'trotting match' at Gailey, north of Wolverhampton, that had attracted a crowd of around three to four hundred people. The road was also lined with about a hundred traps and there were several people on horseback.

Police claimed that the road was being obstructed and that anyone on foot was in danger of being run over. The Bench agreed that there was danger to the public and fined the defendants relatively small amounts, mostly less than one pound each.

Birmingham Daily Post 14th April 1891

Skimming Off The Profits

Edward Thacker, a milk dealer at Carter's Green, West Bromwich received a substantial fine of five pounds plus costs in 1894. He had been selling milk that was "deficient to the extent of 40% of its natural fat".

Birmingham Daily Post 9th October 1894

Bear In The Crowd

Some of the live animal shows held in the 1800's would be unacceptable today, and not just to those with animal welfare concerns. While the threat posed by certain wild animals in these shows would have been obvious, no-one would have anticipated a spectator purposely exposing an audience to such danger. That, however, is precisely what happened at a performing bear show held at West Bromwich High Street in early 1898.

As the show was proceeding, a man among the spectators jumped onto the stage, tore off the muzzle from one of the bears and threw the creature into the crowd! By all accounts a great panic ensued although the only injuries recorded were to the miscreant who caused the pandemonium - one of his hands was badly injured by the poor animal.

Poverty Bay Herald 22nd March 1898

Ladettes

Three girls of about sixteen were each fined twenty shillings plus costs at Wolverhampton Police Court for disturbing the peace by "shouting in Queen Street" on the 5th June 1889. The same event can be witnessed on most nights of the week in the present day.

Birmingham Daily Post 12th June 1889

Meat In The Cellar

Thomas Davis carried on business as a butcher, milk-dealer and beerhouse keeper at Great Bridge Street, West Bromwich. When the local Sanitary Inspector and a policeman visited his premises in 1893, they found three ox tongues in a container in the cellar, that appeared to be perfectly fit for human consumption. Nearby however, they found a tub containing twenty two pieces of meat which were putrid and riddled with maggots. The meat was sent to the Market Hall for examination by the medical officer and was, unsurprisingly, condemned and destroyed.

Davis at first said that the meat, weighing some 100 pounds in total, was good enough for human consumption but later, at the Police Court, said that it was not intended for sale. In fact he said that it had been put there almost a year before and that his family had intended to pickle it and consume it themselves. Then, six months ago the cellar had flooded and a mixture of water and raw sewage had got into the tub, since when it had not been touched.

The justices decided to give Davis the benefit of the doubt and accepted that he did not intend to sell the offending meat but said that he had shown gross carelessness in the conduct of his business.

Birmingham Daily Post 26th May 1893

Retriever's Revenge

After a West Bromwich School Board election in early 1880, six successful Liberal candidates retired to a pub in Spon Lane to celebrate. As the evening wore on and more and more drink was consumed, they decided they needed supper, and one of the party suggested that they should eat a dog!

Accordingly, when a poor retriever cross was spotted from the doorway of the pub, it was enticed in, killed, and prepared for roasting. After cooking for an hour or so, with some of its innards fried separately, the group feasted on the carcass for the remainder of the evening.

The poor mutt had its revenge however, as a number of the men were too ill to work for some time after.

Luton Times and Advertiser (from the Birmingham Gazette) 26th March 1880

Ooops!

Following a Bazaar held to raise funds for schools in Wolverhampton, a Roman Catholic priest and six of the town's most prominent tradesmen were convicted of allowing gambling under a technicality of the Vagrancy Act! There was no fine but they were ordered to pay costs on the understanding that it wouldn't happen again.

Western Daily Press 21st November 1895

The Carnival Of Vice

The tradition of an annual 'wake' goes back many centuries in towns and villages across England. Originally these were festivities with a religious association but as time went on they became much more secular affairs. The Wednesbury Wake was a Monday to Thursday fair held in September each year and it attracted a huge number of people.

In the first part of the century, the fair offered typical working mens entertainment, as revealed by the conviction of a Mr Walker in 1824 for bull-baiting. He was fined five pounds and his accomplice Mr Turner, ten shillings. An advertisement for the Wake in 1868 promised something more benign in a large brass band contest, although the same notice detailed an auction at the Royal Oak, Meeting Street for the land on which three 'refreshment booths' were to be set up.

As the decades wore on, the Wake became less and less salubrious, at least to the minds of the men on the local Board. In 1873 they discussed how the Wake was injurious to local industry because so many working days, and as a consequence wages, were lost. It was estimated that the Patent Shaft works alone paid around £1,000 per day in wages, and the rest of the town's employers combined, probably paid a similar amount, resulting in some £8,000 in lost wages. It was also the habit of visitors to spend money they had saved in the preceding weeks as well as money they anticipated earning in the weeks ahead!

The social aspects were also considered: school attendance plummeted whenever the Darlaston, Moxley or Wednesbury wakes were in progress and this loss of schooling was in addition to a similar situation that occurred each July, when another large fete was jointly organised by many local societies. As noted above, where so many people from the 'lower orders' of society congregated, the risk to health was also considerable; there had been outbreaks of cholera at Tipton and Bilston immediately after the wakes held at those places.

The work of the police was said to be doubled during the Wake, as it attracted depraved characters from across the region and was described as a "carnival of vice". The town was also said to be in a "critical state" for two to three weeks each year following the Wake due to over-indulgence of every sort.

The effect of the Wake upon the populace, especially the young, was considered so bad that efforts were begun to suppress the event and to consider plans for a new town park and free library as wholesome alternative forms of recreation.

The Board were successful in preventing any further wakes but is was fourteen years before Brunswick Park opened and the library did not materialise until 1908.

North Devon Journal (from the Wolverhampton Chronicle) 15th October 1824
Birmingham Daily Post 26th August 1868
Birmingham Daily Post 7th October 1873

Sunday Punch-Up

Two well-known pugilists from Spon Lane, West Bromwich took part in a punishing prize fight on Sunday 30th April 1882. The bare-knuckle contest had run for fifty minutes in front of a large crowd when it was broken up and consequently declared a draw.

Birmingham Daily Post 2nd May 1882

Sharpers At Walsall Races

Walsall had its own racecourse in the nineteenth century which was situated in the angle formed by Bradford Street and Bridgeman Street. Like any large event where people gather and money changes hands, it attracted its fair share of lawbreakers.

Thomas Taylor, of Five Ways, was tried at the Guildhall for passing counterfeit half-sovereigns at a track-side refreshment booth on Tuesday 17th August 1875. He had already passed two coins, each in exchange for a pint of porter (a type of dark beer), and was attempting to buy a third when the fraud was discovered. Taylor ran off but was later arrested at the railway station, where he was once again trying to pass off one of his fakes.

Another man, George Cooper, was sentenced to three weeks plus hard labour for gambling with dice at the races on the same day. When arrested, he had four shillings and threepence all in pennies (a total of fifty one coins) that had clearly been used as stake money.

Birmingham Daily Post 19th August 1875

Spectacular Blaze At Theatre

In September 1895, the theatre connected to the Royal Exchange public house in Paradise Street, West Bromwich was burned down. The fire, which supposedly started accidentally in the manager's room at the public house, completely destroyed the interior of the building and its contents. The remaining walls were in such a precarious condition that traffic in Queen Street was suspended for several days as were services at a nearby Methodist Chapel.

Lincolnshire Echo 9th September 1895

Malpractice At Wolverhampton Races

Wolverhampton racecourse was, like Walsall, the scene of many petty crimes as these cases from just one day at the local Police Court show.

James Grimes of Birmingham was sentenced to six weeks imprisonment with hard labour for gambling with dice. When apprehended he was surrounded by a group of lads betting pennies but he pleaded ignorance of the law in court.

William Farrington, another Birmingham resident, was remanded following the theft of a watch. John Bibb was standing near Farrington when he noticed his watch was missing. He spotted its chain in the hand of the accused but the watch had been detached and passed away to accomplices in the crowd.

James Hadley, yet another Birmingham man and described as disreputable-looking, was charged with stealing six pounds. The victim was in the process of receiving some money in the betting ring when Hadley knocked up his hand and a group of his accomplices quickly picked up six sovereigns from the ground.

Birmingham Gazette 2nd September 1876

Swindlers At Walsall

On the 27th April 1888, two men and a woman were brought up at Walsall Guildhall to face charges of fraudulently obtaining goods from several local tradesmen. One charge was presented in which the two men went to a Park Street grocer and ordered "a nice Wiltshire ham" to be delivered to 69 Lichfield Street, where it would be paid for on receipt. One of two women who lived with the men took the ham and said that Mr Poole (also known as Page or Cartwright) would call to pay for it in the morning, which of course, he did not.

Both men pleaded guilty to the charges, claiming that they were trying to work up a business in the town but that their creditors had closed on them too soon, leaving them unable to pay for the various goods they had ordered. This claim was met with derisive laughter from those in court.

The men were given the maximum possible sentence of three months imprisonment with hard labour. The woman, who purported to be the wife of Poole/Cartwright, was discharged.

Documents found at the Lichfield Street address showed that the swindlers had previously carried on a metal brokering business in Birmingham. Furniture from the house had been whisked away by a Birmingham removal firm and the landlord of the property elected to forego his rent in order to get rid of the fraudsters!

Letters were received from all parts of the country from people who claimed to have been duped by this gang, and the court was said to be thronged by local victims.

Birmingham Daily Post 28th April 1888

Double Tragedy

A travelling theatre company staged a performance of Othello at Walsall on the evening of Friday 17th March 1865. At the end of the third act 'Iago' came in front of the curtain to tell the audience that the play would be temporarily suspended. No sooner had he finished speaking than 'Othello' appeared, in a state of great agitation, and announced that an accident had occurred and the show could not now continue.

The accident was a sudden seizure, probably a heart attack, suffered by a female member of the company, when running after a boy who was trying to get in without paying. The thirty year old woman, Susan Wilson of Birmingham, collapsed and died instantly. It emerged that she had been receiving treatment for a heart condition at Birmingham, and had only joined the company two days beforehand.

The actors, joined by the manager, announced that the evenings takings would be donated to charitable institutions and asked that the audience depart in a quiet and orderly manner.

Western Times 24th March 1865

Bloodsports

Edward Holden, a beer-house keeper of Green Lane appeared at the Walsall Police Court charged with allowing dog-fighting on his premises.

Police had for some time suspected that dog-fights were taking place there, and on 29th June 1869 Sergeant Childs and Constable Blower paid Holden a visit, the sergeant keeping an eye on the back of the property while the constable went inside. Constable Blower tried to make his way upstairs to a large room known as the 'club room' but was impeded by a large number of people rushing down the stairs who had obviously caught wind of the police raid.

Sergeant Childs meanwhile saw a man holding a dog emerge from the 'club room' onto a flat roof where he put the animal down and went back inside. Childs clambered up to retrieve the dog and took it into safe-keeping.

With two other constables, Brewer and Nutt, the sergeant now entered the club room where they found evidence of blood that had been mopped up, the mop and bucket being in the room and the floor still wet. At the rear of the premises, constable Nutt found a second dog inside a workshop and both animals were badly bitten and still bleeding from the face, neck and legs.

Holden was fined twenty shillings and the case put forward to a higher court for consideration.

In 1884 James Husband was fined £2 for cruelty by arranging a cock-fight in a shed at Wednesbury. A number of people were present and wagers were made. The magistrates said they regretted that "this brutal sport has been revived".

Publican Ernest Edward Slim was brought before the West Bromwich magistrates in September 1894 for allowing gaming on his premises. He was fined £10 for arranging a dog-fight at his premises even though the fight never actually took place; the Stipendiary said that Slim would have gone to prison for six months if it had.

Birmingham Daily Post 6th July 1869
Dundee Courier 15th April 1884
Sheffield Evening Telegraph 11th September 1894

Gambling Addict

Although Joseph Francis Smith of Walsall left his wife and four children, the case of neglect brought against him was dismissed, to the applause of those present at court.

Mr Smith had left when he discovered that his wife had been using his earnings, and pawning their possessions, to feed her gambling habit, which apparently involved betting on horse-racing. After he left the family home and took control of his own finances, Smith continued to send her money but she clearly felt that it was insufficient. He made an emotional statement in court and the magistrate said he believed every word Smith said - he told Mrs Smith that she would have a good husband if she would mend her ways.

Gloucester Citizen 22nd November 1894

Caveat Emptor: Squirrel

George Pearce brought a case of 'obtaining goods under false pretences' against travelling draper Edward O'Malley. Wednesbury Petty Sessions heard that O'Malley had called at the Pearce household and tried to get Mrs Pearce to buy a muff and a victorine (a long fur scarf or stole) for twenty two shillings, saying that he had just sold similar items to another lady for three pounds. Mrs Pearce said that as she had no idea of the value of the items offered, she was not interested.

As Mr Pearce was out at the time, O'Malley felt emboldened to walk to the mantelpiece and pick up a watch which, he said he would take in part payment. Mrs Pearce declined the offer but after further pressure from O'Malley, produced two more watches worth over two pounds in total. To these she added ten shillings to complete the bargain, which now included three yards of cloth.

Mr Pearce was not best pleased when he came home, and, describing the deal as a "dead swindle" set off in search of the draper, finally catching up with him at the railway station.

The items of apparel were examined in court and found to be composed of poor quality dried squirrel skins worth no more than a few shillings. However, the case against O'Malley was dismissed as it was deemed to be a commercial contract freely entered into and perfectly legal.

Birmingham Journal 13th December 1862

Salty Beer

At Bilston Police Court, Sarah Page of Wednesbury was fined £10 plus costs for selling adulterated ale - it contained 168 grains of salt per gallon whereas the generally accepted rule-of-thumb limit was fifty grains.

Staffordshire Sentinel 6th May 1875

Dud Money

Job Jones who worked for a Mr Bootle at Perry Barr, was jailed in 1812 for passing off a forged two pound note at Walsall. When apprehended he was in possession of forty seven similar notes which were described as "well executed".

John Wilson was arrested on the Darlaston Road at Wednesbury in 1862 and subsequently appeared at West Bromwich Police Court charged with possessing counterfeit coins with intent to utter them. Wilson had eight coins, wrapped up in a black rag, which were later examined by West Bromwich silversmith James Winkle, who described them as excellent counterfeits. They each appeared to have been cast in the same die, were electro-plated and dated to the reign of George IV (1821).

John Conolly, a fifty eight year old innkeeper of Wednesbury, was sentenced to six months imprisonment for forging and uttering an undertaking (in effect a cheque), to obtain money and thereby defraud.

In 1881 a number of people were sentenced at Stafford for passing base coin at shops throughout Walsall, West Bromwich and Wolverhampton, their usual ploy being to buy a low-priced item and so receive genuine coins as change. The sentences were:

- George Brown, locksmith - five years penal servitude

- Henry Eveson, horse dealer - one year

- John Dean, horse dealer - one year

- Thomas Godfrey, labourer - six months

- George Fuel, slater - six months

- John Farley, boatman - six months

- Ann Davis , "a bad character" - six months

Chester Chronicle 28th February 1812
Birmingham Daily Post 10th March 1862
Staffordshire Sentinel 24th July 1874
Sheffield Independent 28th January 1881

Misdemeanours and Mayhem

Chapter 4

In this chapter we look at reports of criminal activity, from petty theft and anti-social behaviour to the most serious offences of rape and attempted murder. For good measure, a selection of reports detailing general mayhem created by people, animals and vehicles is also included.

While some of the stories have a comic element to them, some are desperately sad and others are truly shocking. In many cases one has to admire the bravery and tenacity of the police force of the day in following up and tracking down offenders, often at great risk to themselves.

Garroting

London was seized by panic in the 1850's and 60's by the actions of gangs using garrotes to disable and rob their victims, but this method of mugging was not exclusive to the capital.

In September 1859 a man and woman acted together to attack Robert Podmore at Bilston. James Sparrow, a twenty two year old iron puddler, seized him by the throat, while the pair rifled his pockets and stole £1 15s. Sparrow and his accomplice Sarah Ann Birch, also twenty two, were later apprehended thanks to the description given by Podmore. The pair received twelve months imprisonment with hard labour.

In December 1866 three men were sentenced to a term of imprisonment and flogging, following a similar attack on one Thomas Broadbent at Wolverhampton.

Surprisingly perhaps, William Perry, the celebrated pugilist known as "The Tipton Slasher", was knocked down, garrotted and robbed of £92 by three men at Wednesbury in July 1863.

Birmingham Daily Post 20th October 1859
Western Gazette 4th July 1863
Chester Chronicle 8th December 1866

Riot At The Brickworks

In April 1858, a gang of around eight to ten individuals assaulted the Jobbern and Arrowsmith brick and tile works near Walsall. They broke into the works around nine o'clock in the evening and began destroying bricks and tiles. When some employees tried to stop the gang, firearms were discharged and one man was seriously injured.

They adjoining premises of W J Biddow were also attacked and extensively damaged. At the time of the report the identity and motive of the attackers was unknown.

Bury Times 17th April 1858

Copper in The Cut

A man named Pye, who had set a bulldog onto a woman at Bentley, was taken into custody by Constable George Clarke. Within a short time however, Pye was released by a gang of men who set about Clarke and pushed him off a bridge into the canal, twelve feet below.

A man named Bayley, who took part in the assault, was sentenced to six months imprisonment with hard labour. A week later, his brother, George Bayley, and another man, Samson Boone stood accused of involvement in the same assault. According to Clarke, George Bayley was one of those who had pushed him off the bridge and Boone had struck him as he was climbing out of the canal, knocking him back in. Both, it was alleged were among the group that had kicked and punched the constable, both before and after he was pushed into the water.

Mrs Cooper, the victim of the dog attack, backed up the officer's story, as did a man named Vaughan who had tried to intervene but was prevented from doing so by Bayley.

The Stipendiary said that it was shocking that a group of men calling themselves Englishmen should join in such a brutal attack upon a man who was merely doing his duty. Bayley received six months with hard labour and Boone three months, to follow the seven days imposed for damage done at the Nag's Head public house at Darlaston Green.

Birmingham Daily Post 15th May 1872

Keep Your Pot

At the Petty Sessions at West Bromwich in early August 1862, an elderly lady, Eliza Nicholls, was charged with stealing an iron pot belonging to her neighbour, Anna Harrison. Nicholls claimed she had bought the pot two years before and, as proof was not forthcoming to the contrary, the case was dismissed.

Mr Nicholls however, did not get off so lightly - he was fined 5 shillings plus costs, or fourteen days in prison, for assaulting Constable McCrohan, the officer who had arrested his wife!

Birmingham Daily Post 14th August 1862

Poaching At Pendeford

Three Willenhall men were caught while poaching in a stubble field at Pendeford. Two of the men initially evaded the pursuing police and gamekeepers, but Lloyd Morris was captured. He had seven rabbits, a hare and about 300 yards of netting in his possession. The other two men were captured later, Edward Williams at home and Benjamin Adey in a public house.

While Williams and Morris had previous convictions for poaching, it was thought that Adey, who was given a good reference by his employer, had only just joined them. In an attempt to get him back on the 'straight and narrow' he was given a sentence of two months. At the end of this term he was required to find sureties and abstain from poaching on pain of a longer sentence. The other two were given three month terms and also required to find sureties to guarantee their good behaviour in future.

Birmingham Daily Post 15th October 1863

Simple Neglect

It was a late January day in 1892, and it had been raining for some time, when a young boy was spotted knocking on doors in New Street, West Bromwich, by a local constable. The lad ran away but was soon caught by the policeman who noted that there was barely anything left of the boy's shoes. The child said he was begging because his father wouldn't give him anything to eat.

Although unthinkable in this day and age, nine-year old William Stanton of Hall Street was charged at the Police Court with begging. The officer told how he had visited the lad's home and found it to be very dirty, with nothing but half a pound of bread to eat. In court, the father claimed he did not know that his son was begging, while Mrs Stanton said she thought her son was at school. The magistrate discharged the boy, saying it was clear that he had been neglected, despite his father earning around seven shillings a day. He warned both parents that they each faced three months in prison if they failed to look after their son in future.

Birmingham Daily Post 12th February 1892

Tea Leaf

One Sunday morning, police officer Foxall was walking along the Bloxwich Road in Walsall when he spotted a suspicious character with a bag over his shoulder. He followed the man for a while before stopping him and asking to see the contents of the bag. The man, whose name was Garner, first said he had been shopping but when the bag was found to contain eight two-pound packets and three one-pound packets of fine tea, he changed his story, saying that he had found them under a hedge, somewhere between Birmingham and Wolverhampton. He subsequently changed his story once more, saying that two men had paid him to carry the tea to Rugeley.

Foxall took the man into custody and made enquiries at Rugeley but could find no-one matching the descriptions Garner had provided. The officer then began an enquiry to see if the goods were stolen and he was visited the following day by a clerk from Pickford and Co at Wolverhampton. The man identified the packets as some of those stolen from a chest that had been broken open while on a canal boat. Garner was taken to Wolverhampton and committed for trial.

Staffordshire Gazette and County Standard 18th February 1841

Funny Faces

Three youths were brought before the bench in August 1862 charged with obstructing the footpath in Coppice Street, Wednesbury. By all accounts, the usual practice of this notorious gang of loiterers was to hang around the footpath on Sunday evenings and annoy passers-by with obscene expressions!

Edward Hayes, Edward Cartwright and Daniel Sheepy were each fined ten shillings plus costs or two weeks in prison in default.

Birmingham Daily Post 14th August 1862

Dispute, Destruction, Delay

In May 1883 there was a break-in at Mr Oldbury's coach and axle works at Wednesbury. Nothing was stolen but all of the leather belts that connected individual machines to the factory's main drive-shaft were destroyed.

As a result of the vandalism, almost 100 employees were unable to start work for several hours on the next day. A member of the workforce was suspected as there was ill-feeling between the men and the works manager.

Worcestershire Chronicle 12th May 1883

The Great Walsall Robbery

One day in October 1869, the Walsall solicitors Duignan, Lewis & Lewis had on their premises a considerable amount of money and valuables as a result of transactions conducted at Birmingham. The cash, bankers draft and gold, totalling some £940, was parcelled up and locked in the safe for banking the next day.

On the following day, the cashier, a Mr Bytheway, took the parcel from the safe and put it in his desk ready to take to the bank. A short while later he was called away, leaving two clerks in the office, Mr Heath and a young man named Samuel Thompson. A little while after the cashier had left, Mr Heath also left the office.

Upon his return, Bytheway found that the money had disappeared from the draw. When questioned, Thompson said that he had left the office for a few minutes after Heath and that must have been when the parcel was stolen. The police were informed immediately and a substantial reward of £50 was offered for the arrest of the thieves.

Everything at the office continued as usual until the following Saturday, the 13th of November, when Thompson didn't turn up for work, but nothing unusual was thought of it. On the Monday, Thompson still didn't arrive for work and later that day his father contacted the office to say that his son had told him that he was going to town on Saturday on the solicitor's business.

The alarms bells now began to ring, and even more so when it was discovered that Thompson's friend Simpson was also missing. When enquiries revealed that the youths had taken a train for London, Simpson senior set off in pursuit and managed to ascertain that they had booked passage on a Melbourne bound ship; he also discovered the lodgings in which they were staying but they were not there when he visited. When the young men returned to their lodgings they were told that someone was looking for them. They now changed their plans and travelled by train directly to Birkenhead.

The following Friday the pair entered the Woodside Vaults at Birkenhead at around ten in the evening and stayed until around midnight. A fellow customer who was reading a newspaper, thought he recognised the pair from descriptions in an article, and followed them when they left. When he reached the Woodside Ferry, he informed a policeman of his suspicions. The constable didn't think anything was amiss and let the lads continue through the ferry gate. However, a second officer, Inspector Davenport, decided that he would question them, at which point Simpson pulled a bag from his pocket and threw it into the water. Thompson also tried to throw something away but was prevented from doing so.

The officers now took the youths into a room where they were charged with the theft and searched. Simpson was found to have little of value but Thompson was carrying over £38 in cash and other items from the parcel.

The pair were taken into custody but while being escorted to the station, Thompson managed to wriggle out of his cape, which was in the grip of Inspector Davenport, and escape. In a scene reminiscent of the Keystone Cops, Davenport gave chase, but only after divesting himself of his coat containing the recovered money. At this point a man appeared from around a corner, grabbed the coat and tried to make off with it but he was stopped by Whereat, the other policeman, who also had charge of Simpson! Simpson was duly incarcerated but Thompson, for the time being, disappeared.

On Sunday, acting on information received, Detective Sergeant Wood travelled to Chester. The next day he and Detective Sergeant Drury lay in hiding at the post office, where before long, Thompson appeared to collect some letters. He was arrested, locked up at Chester and later taken back to Walsall by the two officers.

Thompson and Simpson, both aged 16, faced trial at the Walsall Quarter Sessions the following January where both pleaded guilty. It was stated in court that Thompson had been well educated at Walsall Grammar School and had otherwise been of excellent character. Simpson likewise was given good character references by two clergymen.

In their defence it was said that both prisoners had been reading 'trashy novels' and 'sensational publications' which had perverted their minds! They had originally formed a plan to go to Australia and were prepared to commit a crime if necessary to finance the voyage. When Thompson was presented with the opportunity of the parcel he acted impulsively - he took the parcel to Simpson where they hid it in the coal-place in the schoolyard, and later, in Simpson's fowl pen at home.

The case created huge interest and crowds at the trial, and was known as the 'Walsall Robbery Romance'. Divers were employed to retrieve the bag thrown into the water at Birkenhead but whether or not it was recovered is not reported. The boys received a nine month prison sentence for their adventure.

Lancaster Gazette 20th November 1869
Liverpool Mercury 27th November 1869
Birmingham Daily Post 13th January 1870

Wolverhampton Irish Protest

On the evening of Tuesday 29th June 1858, around 3,000 Irish people surrounded the Corn Exchange in Wolverhampton. Many of them had been at the same place the night before, when they had successfully drowned out a lecture on "The Popish Priesthood" held within.

This time the protest was more forceful - as soon as the lecture began, a hail of stones broke every window in the building, causing the lecture to be postponed once more. The mayor, who was a guest at the lecture, read the riot act and two people were arrested.

On Wednesday the county's Chief Constable and 140 of his men arrived and the lecture was finally delivered, despite the 5,000 strong mob outside who now acted peaceably.

Manchester Courier and Lancashire General Advertiser 3rd July 1858

Old Smokey

James Davenport was the engine stoker at Boys timber merchants of Bradford Street, Walsall. On 23rd June 1884 he was fined five shillings and costs, or six days imprisonment, for allowing black smoke to appear from the stack connected to 'his' engine.

Birmingham Daily Post 24th June 1884

Moor Street Mayhem

John Stackhouse, a miner in his mid forties, lived with his wife Elizabeth and their family at Great Bridge. In the summer of 1897 the couple separated; he went to live at Cophall Street, Greets Green, and she to Moor Street, West Bromwich, where she also took in a lodger, James Rose.

One night in December, Stackhouse visited his wife and just after eleven o'clock he attacked Rose with a clasp-knife, stabbing him over one eye and in the neck and cheek. His wife, who was in the backyard at the time, rushed inside whereupon he also attacked her, plunging the knife into her chest. Despite being badly wounded, she was able to run into the street to call for help and was taken to the District Hospital. Sergeant Howell was despatched to investigate the attacks and while he was at the hospital, Stackhouse arrived, in the company of his brother, with a bandaged head. This seems to have been an attempt to make out that he was also a victim in the affray, but it was soon discovered that he had no injuries and he was therefore arrested.

Presumably Stackhouse was found guilty of these attacks as he is listed on the 1901 census as a convict at Parkhurst Prison on the Isle of Wight. Elizabeth Stackhouse died three years after the attack, aged forty five.

Birmingham Daily Post 20th December 1897
1901 census RG13 piece 1022 folio 127 page 28
Registry of deaths Dec 1900 West Bromwich 6b 566

Trouser Trouble

Henry Lawrence of Stafford Street, Walsall was fined ten shillings plus costs for being drunk and disorderly outside the Earl Grey Inn. He assaulted the constable who was sent to deal with him as well as a young man who came to help. In addition to the fine he was ordered to pay a further ten shillings for damage done to the man's trousers!

Birmingham Daily Post 16th September 1890

Wood Green Poachers

Two men who were poaching at Wood Green, Wednesbury in November 1877, made off in the direction of land near Bescot Railway Station after being spotted by a bailiff. They were intercepted by George Adams, a gamekeeper, but the two men refused to give themselves up and set about him using a gun and a ram-rod to beat him. Adams' skull was seriously fractured and several of his teeth were knocked out in the attack.

One of the men, 20 year old Thomas Pratt of St James' Street, was later arrested but the other was still at large at the time of the report.

Birmingham Daily Post 2nd November 1877

Trying It On

Edward Guest was in a West Bromwich beer house on the night of 19th September 1868 when, he alleged, he was assaulted and robbed by Joseph and Benjamin Davis.

Guest claimed that one of the men picked up his pot of ale and drank it, knocked over a second pot then set about him, knocking him senseless. When he came to, he found he had lost seven shillings from his pocket.

At the trial, the defense proved that Guest was drunk and before the assault had actually told several people that he had no more money! The accused were acquitted.

Birmingham Daily Post 15th March 1869

Unveiled Threat

Thomas Butler aged 34 of Smith Street, West Bromwich, received three months imprisonment plus hard labour, for stealing various goods from Walsall Street milkman Joseph Botham. As the prisoner was led away he shouted that he would give Mr Botham "a trimming" when he was released. Whether Botham ever got the 'haircut' he was promised is not known.

Birmingham Daily Post 25th June 1883

Feeble Excuse

At Wednesbury Police Court in April 1891, twenty five year old Thomas Jennings was charged with being drunk and disorderly and with assaulting one Hannah Beston. To the laughter of the court, Jennings claimed that it was a 'put-up job' that had only come to court because constable Colclough, the arresting officer, was courting Beston! He was fined 15 shillings plus costs in total.

Birmingham Daily Post 14th April 1891

Fruit Feast

Thirteen lads, variously aged between eleven and sixteen, were brought before the Wednesbury Police Court in December 1882 charged with stealing a large quantity of fruit and vegetables from a warehouse in Ridding Lane.

They had entered the warehouse on both nights of the weekend and eaten a large quantity of apples, oranges, grapes and nuts! Sergeant Curtis had seen most of the perpetrators in the vicinity of the warehouse on Sunday evening and was trying to catch them, but by carefully watching his movements they were able to continue gorging themselves uninterrupted. The value of food consumed was put at just over £5.

All but one of the defendants were found guilty, the younger ones received six strokes of the birch and the older were variously fined according to their previous conduct. All of them were said to be poorly clad and in a state of neglect.

Birmingham Daily Post 20th December 1882

West Bromwich Railway Robbery

During 1882 there were a large number of thefts from the GWR Goods Station at West Bromwich, and in December of that year, at least two of those responsible were brought to book having been under suspicion for a little while.

Twenty six year olds Dennis Woodward, a yardsman of Loveday Street, and William Smith, a signalman of Halford Lane, were found guilty of the theft of six bottles of wine. The case containing the wine was packed and sealed in London and, destined for a Mr Morris at Great Bridge, had been placed on the goods platform. It was broken into overnight and the six bottles stolen.

James Waters, a watchman at the station, said he saw Woodward on the goods platform around a quarter to eleven at night and saw Smith near the goods shed just before midnight. The following day Smith was questioned by police and said that Woodward had brought four bottles of wine to him in the signal box, claiming that he had won them in a raffle. He asked Smith to look after the bottles so he placed them in his locker.

A police search of Woodward's home revealed another bottle, hidden in a clothes basket, which he admitted to taking from the 'deck', i.e. the platform.

The stationmaster said that Smith had been under his supervision for over two years and had always been trustworthy. Nevertheless, both men were sentenced to three months imprisonment with hard labour.

Liverpool Mercury 25th December 1882

Walsall Lock-Ins

At the Walsall Petty Sessions, Henry Beech, landlord of the Coach and Horses in Ablewell Street, was fined 20 shillings for serving drink after hours. He claimed that a member of a party celebrating an election victory had bought a bottle of drink before midnight, and that they had therefore remained to drink it.

He was also charged with harbouring the nameless 'Constable 23' while on duty. At around three in the morning two police officers attempted to enter the establishment but it took them a quarter of an hour to gain access and, in the meantime, they spotted '23' leaving by the back door!

The defence claimed that '23' had visited the house and, while he was turning out the party, the other officers had arrived. The Bench fined him ten shillings and the landlady (rather than Beech) twenty shillings both plus costs.

At the same sessions, Phineas Clark, landlord of the 'Cricket Ball', Green Lane, was fined ten shillings after four men were found in his beer-house at 3am in a state of intoxication and hidden behind some barrels!

Birmingham Daily Gazette 1st December 1865

A Nasty Character

Joseph Hill, a twenty eight year old axletree maker from Wednesbury, was sentenced to 10 years penal servitude in 1859, for a vicious attack on his considerably older brother in law, John Malone.

For reasons unclear, Hill came into Malone's house at four in the afternoon and struck him on the head. He then got Malone to the floor and proceeded to hold his head over the fire, with his neck across the fender, while he grasped around for the poker with which he intended to rake coals onto the older man's head! Not finding this, he instead grabbed a kettle of boiling water and proceeded to pour it over the poor man's head, face and neck, then continued to hold his head over the fire.

It emerged that Hill was on a 'ticket of leave' (a form of parole), having been transported for rape eleven years earlier.

Western Daily Press 8th December 1859

Eight Man Brawl

A fight between eight men took place during the evening of Saturday 1st March 1862 at Workhouse Lane, near Queen Street, Wednesbury. The complainants were three brothers, Thomas, Michael and John Maloy, the latter of whom owned a beer shop on Holyhead Road.

It was alleged that one of the five defendants insulted, and tried to trip up, a young female relative who was with the three brothers as they walked along. A row broke out that quickly escalated into a violent brawl, in which the outnumbered Maloys came off worst. Two of the brothers ended up with nasty cuts and black eyes but John was so badly injured that he was unable to attend court.

After 'much hard swearing' in court, the case was adjudged to be proven against all the defendants and they were variously fined, with the case relating to the attack on John Maloy to be heard at a later date.

Birmingham Daily Post 7th March 1862

Elwell's Pool Assault

A particularly brutal assault on police constable James Asbury of Wednesbury, took place at Elwell's Pool, Wood Green in 1865. Asbury was walking with two other men towards Walsall, and although not in uniform, he was recognised as a policeman by one of the five other men at the scene. This man encouraged his comrades to attack Asbury, who was then stoned, kicked and punched, beaten with his own truncheon and finally stabbed in the thigh and lower back. Throughout the attack, Asbury had valiantly tried to bring his handcuffs into play, while his companions had struggled to pull the attackers away.

At the trial in July, the evidence against two of the defendants, brothers John and James Kelly was inconclusive and they were acquitted. The others, Malone, Devaney and Griffin each received five years penal servitude.

Birmingham Daily Post 27th July 1865

Tipton Green Rogue

William Johnson was a young man who ran a prize stall at the Tipton Green Wake in 1865. Johnson's offering was similar to the typical 'hook a duck' or target shooting stall, but in his case, customers would spin an iron pointer and win whatever object this needle pointed at when it stopped.

However, it was discovered that Johnson had stacked the odds in his favour by the simple expedient of covertly attaching a string to the pointer, enabling him to bring it to a halt wherever he wished!

At the Police Court he was described as a 'rogue and vagabond' and received six weeks with hard labour for the deception.

Birmingham Daily Post 27th July 1865

Half-Hearted Suicide Attempt

In the 19th century, suicide was a criminal act, and anyone who attempted it and failed would most likely be prosecuted just to add to their woes! Twenty year old Samuel Atkins of Walsall Street, West Bromwich, presented just such a case, but he escaped with a rebuke from the magistrate who told him not to act so foolishly in future.

Atkins had parted with his sweetheart on bad terms one evening and when he got home, wrote a letter to her and asked his step-mother to post it. He left the house briefly and returned with a cut to his throat, although it wasn't at all serious. When arrested he said that he had been driven to it by his sister, who had been telling lies about him to his girlfriend!

Huddersfield Chronicle 11th January 1899

Porter Punched

William Thomas, a grocer's porter, brought an assault case against his employer, Alfred William Powell of Bilston Street, Bradley. He claimed, and his master did not deny, that Powell had "clouted his ears". Powell's justification was that Thomas had taken far too long on an errand and been impudent. Five shillings plus costs was the fine and, one would imagine, Thomas forfeited his job.

Birmingham Daily Post 20th December 1890

Cow About Town

A cow belonging to Mr Caddick, a Bilston butcher, created an hour of chaos in Wolverhampton town one November evening in 1891. After getting away from it's handlers it charged down Queen Street and tossed a man through the plate glass window of Edwin Darley's wine shop in Dudley Street. The unfortunate victim, Thomas Perry of Bishop Street, was severely lacerated about the head and face and needed hospital treatment.

The cow was not finished however; it continued to run amok until it reached Horseley Fields, where it broke the windows of Weaver's boot shop and the Horseley Fields Tavern.

Birmingham Daily Post 11th November 1891

Beaten For Looking After Her Child

Thomas Beard, a lock maker of Bloxwich, was sentenced to three months plus hard labour for brutally beating his wife and thirteen month old child.

On Saturday 6th May 1882, Beard was drinking at the Rising Sun Inn. His wife sent word to him several times to ask for money to buy milk for their baby who was unwell, but when she received none she went in person with the child. Beard hit her in the face with a jug then assaulted both wife and child in a most shocking manner.

Birmingham Daily Post 11th May 1882

Taken For A Ride

The first bicycles to resemble present day machines appeared on our streets in the mid 1880's, and within a very few years, factories and shops were springing up in towns everywhere. Edward Lyall was one of the new breed of cycle makers, with a business at Stewart Street, Blakenhall, Wolverhampton.

In 1889, one of his employees, Philip Henry Middleton of Poultney Street, was charged at the Police Court with the theft of fittings from Mr Lyall's business. Some of the parts were discovered at Middleton's lodgings and some at his mother's house in Birmingham.

As Middleton had previously been of good character and Lyall did not wish to press charges, the young man got off lightly with a £2 fine.

Birmingham Daily Post 27th May 1889

Wheat Sheaf Thief

In September 1890, John James Knock of Lambert's End, West Bromwich, was fined twenty four shillings for stealing a sheaf of wheat worth sixpence. Knock was spotted in a field, the property of Stephen Simms of Carter's Green, which was adjacent to Tantany Colliery. He was seen to run off with the wheat but was later captured.

Birmingham Daily Post 16th September 1890

Railway Ripped Off

Eliza Walker of Broad Lands, Bilston, presented herself to the Bilston station master, Mr Owen, claiming that her bruised face and black eyes were the result of the railway accident there on 10th August 1864. She duly received £1 in compensation from Mr Owen on behalf of the Great Western Railway.

It seems certain however that Walker had succeeded in defrauding the GWR, as she told several witnesses that her injuries had been caused by her husband while they were at Wolverhampton racecourse during the afternoon. A witness at the subsequent trial said walker told her that "it was hiss fisses as hurt me", after she refused to give him any more money

On the day after the accident, another witness who was visiting them heard Walker's husband suggest that his wife went to the doctor and "put it on the railway company", which she duly did. Other witnesses testified that Mrs Walker had told them that she wasn't even on the train that was involved in the accident, she had actually travelled on the earlier one!

Because of lack of proof, the prosecution in the end decided not to proceed with the case, but it seems that the Stipendiary seemed to know where the truth lay, as when the defence applied for costs, he suggested the solicitor take up the matter with his client.

Birmingham Daily Post 24th September 1864

Man Swaps Children For Boots

George Genders and his two children lodged with labourer John Owen at his house in Green Lane, Walsall. One morning Genders got up early, put on Owen's boots, discarded his own and decamped. He was arrested at Stone, north of Stafford, but didn't deny the theft, saying that the boots were better than his own and that he wasn't going on the road wearing an old pair.

Better yet, Genders had left his children in the care of sixty four year old Mr Owen and his wife. He received fourteen days plus hard labour for his impudence!

Birmingham Daily Post 15th October 1892

Drunk Driver, Repeat Offender

William Tew of Stafford Street was fined 40 shillings for being drunk in charge of a horse and trap and driving furiously through Lichfield Street, Walsall in December 1890.

At the same court Patrick Ford of Rushall Street was given twenty one days hard labour for being drunk and disorderly, an offense for which he had many previous convictions!

Birmingham Daily Post 20th December 1890

Gang Rape At Pelsall

Four young coal miners were charged with the brutal rape of a widow at Pelsall in July 1863. The woman, Mary Ann Brice, lived at Wednesbury but made a living by hawking tinware throughout the towns of the Black Country.

She and Margaret Brice, who made her living in the same way, were inebriated when they entered a public house at Pelsall. In her evidence, Margaret Brice said she saw Mary Ann walk out in the company of five or six men, and a little while later, Mrs Wiggins, the landlady and mother of one of the accused, said that Brice was in the yard with a group of single and married men. When the witness went into the yard she saw one man on top of the woman and five men looking on. When Brice tried to get to her feet one of the men hit her in the face.

The witness told the court that Mrs Wiggins said she didn't care what happened to the woman, as long as the men left her yard. At that point they took Brice to an empty house, where the assault continued. A little later the witness saw the victim with another man in a pig sty, while a group of men looked on. The wife of one of the men, a Mrs Rogers, threw a bucket of water over the victim.

Three other witnesses who came to investigate the woman's screams of "murder" saw Durkins with the woman in the empty house, and later, Thomas with her in an outhouse. One witness said Rogers' wife kicked the victim, and that Wiggins' father also threw a bucket of water over her.

In the end the men threatened to throw Brice into the canal, at which point she passed out and remained unconscious until the next day. When she came to, Brice set off on foot for Walsall but was so ill that the four mile journey took four hours. Within a couple of days she was admitted to the Workhouse at Walsall and was still an inmate there at the time of the trial.

In his summing up the judge declared that it was one of the grossest cases he had ever had to hear and sentenced each of the four men, John Rogers, Richard Wiggins, Thomas Allen and John Durkins to fifteen years penal servitude.

The parents, wife and others who were complicit in this brutal outrage seem to have escaped scot-free.

Leicester Journal 31st July 1863
Lloyds Weekly London Newspaper 2nd August 1863

Sticky Fingers

The youthful Wednesbury fruit thieves mentioned above, had their counterparts at West Bromwich in the following year, although it is not known whether this gang had chance to enjoy their ill-gotten gains.

At around 3.30am on 17th June, three lads took down the shutters on Benjamin Hadley's shop at Spon Lane and broke a window. They then proceeded to steal a selection of sweets and 'Lucky Bags' valued in total at 'one and six'. The antics of George Winter (13), William Pemberton (14) and Joseph Clarke (14) were observed by Thomas Morris, an engineer on his way to work, and the sweet-toothed scoundrels were each fined ten shillings or, in default, seven days in prison.

Birmingham Daily Post 25th June 1883

Making A Stink

James Bannister, a Great Barr farmer, was fined 5 shillings plus costs for allowing 'nightsoil' to be removed from Stafford Street, Walsall during prohibited hours. The contents of privies and cesspools, which were used as fertilizer on surrounding fields, could only legally be emptied at night, hence the name.

Birmingham Daily Post 16th March 1886

Hush Money

Edward Bennett, landlord of the Dog and Duck Inn, Pipers Row, Wolverhampton, seems to have been a despicable character. It was alleged that he was prepared to accept £10 'hush money', to ignore an indecent assault on his own twelve year old daughter, by a 43 year old man.

Thomas Holt, who worked at the General Post Office as a letter sorter, was the only customer in the bar of the Inn on the day in question. Little Phoebe Bennett served him some ale, at which point he interfered with her, and she duly reported this to her father.

According to Holt, Bennett told him that he did not wish to see Holt's reputation damaged, and would therefore accept £10 from him to forget about the incident, although he had to clear this arrangement with his wife first!

Holt who was fearful of losing his job and facing such a charge charge, offered 50 shillings the next day and said he would pay no more but Bennett refused this and a prosecution was commenced.

Although there was some doubt about the allegation itself, the jury found Holt guilty and he was sentenced to 12 months hard labour.

Birmingham Daily Post 8th February 1886

A Poor Boy

There are numerous reports of people who have been wronged deciding that they do not wish to proceed with a prosecution once the personal circumstances of the offender come to light. One such case happened when ten year old Thomas Mannion of Rushall Street, Walsall was brought up on a charge of stealing a cap. The theft took place at Frank Keep's shop at Digbeth in September 1890. The boy, who was raggedly dressed and in a "deplorable condition", was one of six children, their father having been out of work for some time due to an accident.

Although Mr Keep did not wish to prosecute, the lad was sent to the Workhouse for a week, presumably to demonstrate the error of his ways.

Birmingham Daily Post 16th September 1890

Indecent Assault At West Bromwich

Josiah Tonge, a High Street barber, did not appear in response to a court summons to answer a charge of indecent assault, and, as a consequence, an arrest warrant was issued.

Tonge lived with his wife and five children and a young domestic servant, Charlotte Moore, against whom the offense was committed. The young girl alleged that one morning in August 1871, Tonge entered her room, pulled back her bedclothes and exposed himself to her.

When he was arrested, Tonge claimed that he had been 'deceived' by the girl, and that his wife was going to meet her at Paradise Street to straighten things out. In court his defense counsel complained that Tonge was not allowed to give his version of events or to call his wife as a witness. Charlotte was described by the magistrate as as a very straightforward girl and he found her testimony remarkably clear, truthful and compelling.

As a result, Tonge was fined £10 with three months in prison in default; a remarkable contrast to the sentence handed out to Thomas Holt in the Wolverhampton case fifteen years later.

Note: On the 1871 census the relevant surnames are spelled Tongue and Moor.

Birmingham Daily Post 29th August 1871

Tumbler Jack

Wednesbury and West Bromwich had a number of gun-lock makers in the nineteenth century and the firing mechanisms that they made were shipped to other businesses for incorporation into pistols, shotguns and so forth.

Thomas Turner manufactured gun-locks at Kings Hill, Wednesbury, and on Christmas Eve 1864 he had a stock of around 600 musket locks packed into hampers ready for shipping. However, an inspection of his premises on Christmas Day showed that he had suffered a break-in and about 500 of his locks had been stolen.

Turner must have suspected the culprit and the destination of the stolen property, as he went straight to the house of Mr Jenks in Ormond Street, Birmingham where, in the company of a police officer, he found nine of his locks amongst two hundred others stashed upstairs. Jenks said that he had purchased the locks off John Smith alias 'Tumbler Jack', a man who was from time to time employed by Turner in filing the tumbler mechanism in his locks.

Whether by chance or appointment, 'Tumbler Jack' arrived at the house soon after, at which point he was taken into custody by Sergeant Fenner. In time honoured fashion, Smith claimed he had bought the locks off a man in a public house but couldn't recall which it was. He was committed for trial at West Bromwich Police Court but the outcome is not recorded.

Birmingham Daily Gazette 30th January 1865

Collared

A similar case to that of 'Tumbler Jack' happened a year or so later at Walsall, and involved James Kendrick of Station Street. Kendrick, a horse-collar maker, stole two collars from his employers, Bingham and Trees. He took them to one George Perrins, saying that he had made them but didn't want his employers to know he had been working for himself. Perrins sold them on to a Mr Gough of Park Street for twelve shillings.

When Kendrick was 'collared' he didn't try the 'bought them off a man in the pub' defence but instead admitted his guilt and was duly sentenced to three months in prison.

Birmingham Daily Post 14th June 1866

A Memorable Name

John Arkinstall who lived in one of the 'court' houses at Warwick Street, Wolverhampton, had been drinking to excess in the Grand Turk at Horseley Fields. When the manager, John Mansell, tried to eject him from the premises he was assaulted, and a warrant was subsequently issued for Arkinstall's arrest.

Almost two years later, Arkinstall went to the Bilston Police Office to bail out a friend. A detective who overheard Arkinstall giving his name remembered that a warrant for the man was out in Wolverhampton, so he told Arkinstall to call back later in the day to deal with the bail. In the interim the details were checked with Wolverhampton and upon his return the villain was arrested.

Birmingham Daily Post 16th September 1890

Love And Suicide

Joseph Norman was in love with Lucy Evans, the girl next door to his lodgings at Holloway Bank, Wednesbury. He showered her with gifts and had even started making plans for their wedding, which he had set for November 1873, but unfortunately his love was unrequited. She had even been quite cold towards him of late and as a result, he had on more than one occasion threatened to take his own life if she refused to become his wife.

On the evening before he carried through his threat, he had met Lucy walking back from the Wednesbury Wakes with another young man. Norman wished her goodnight but she made no reply until she had walked a little further at which point she turned around and called "Joe, are you going to hang yourself?"

Joseph Norman was in very low spirits that evening and during the next morning, despite the best efforts of Mr and Mrs Craddock, in whose house he lodged, to cheer him up. Later that morning the Craddocks left Norman at home while they went shopping. On their return they found the door locked and Mr Craddock had to get in via a bedroom window. He found

Norman hanging in the stairwell and although medical assistance was called for urgently, the young man had expired by the time he was cut down.

Although she may not have expected him to carry through his threat, Lucy Evans was rebuked by coroner and jury alike at the inquest, where she was described as having acted in a most abominable and heartless manner. The jury returned a verdict of suicide while in a state of temporary insanity.

North Devon Journal 19th September 1872

A Fool And His Money

Twenty eight year old Emma Pugh of Russell Street, Walsall was a "woman of ill fame" and in September 1870 she was plying her trade at Wednesbury, where the Wake was in full swing. One customer was Henry Pearson of Long Itchington, Warwickshire, who, being much the worse for drink, went with her to a cottage where he paid her ten shillings.

Afterwards he noticed that his pocket watch and a sovereign were missing and he charged her with having stolen them. At West Bromwich Police Court she denied the charge and claimed that he had given her the watch. A witness was produced who backed up her story and another witness told how she had even tried to give it back to him. Case dismissed.

Birmingham Daily Post 13th September 1870

Helping Themselves To Fodder

The cost of horse fodder at Davis Bros & Co of Cannock Road, Wolverhampton, had increased by twenty five percent in four months, even though there had been no increase in the price of hay or corn and the number of horses had remained constant. It wasn't until employees John Wilbery and John Wood were spotted making off with a truss of hay and a bag of corn that the reason came to light. They each received three months hard labour for the theft.

Birmingham Daily Post 14th January 1880

Over-Zealous Debt Collector

Scotch drapers were to be found in many English towns in the eighteen-hundreds. They were predominantly Scottish men who would work a 'round' with their horse and cart, selling woollen cloth to regular customers on credit.

Thirty five year old Martin Carty was a collector working for one such draper in Wolverhampton. In 1893 he called to collect payment from Jane Barrett, a widow of Grimstone Street, Springfields. She found his conduct so bad that she complained to his employer following which Carty returned and assaulted her. His violent behaviour earned him a twenty shillings fine when he was brought before the Police Court in June.

Birmingham Daily Post 10th June 1893

Bird Boy Punished

In 1893, five year old Michael Cane of Burrowes Street was brought up at the Guildhall, Walsall for keeping two young larks in captivity, in contravention of the Wild Birds Protection Act. The little mite was fined 20 shillings or twenty one days in prison.

Birmingham Daily Post 10th June 1893

Distraction Theft

James Killean of Orlando Street, Walsall was at the railway station seeing off a friend when a young man approached him, held up a handkerchief in front of Mr Killean's face and grabbed his silver pocket watch. Fortunately the distraction was momentary and he managed to grab the thief and hold on to him until a policeman arrived, despite being set upon by the felon's companions. The thief, John Corbett, was committed for trial at Stafford in 1875.

Birmingham Daily Post 19th August 1875

No Honeymoon

Thomas Leicester, an ironworker, got married on the morning of Monday 23rd November 1874. On the evening of that day he was arrested for being drunk and disorderly and exposing himself to one Mrs Bagot, a licensed victualler. At Wednesbury Police court three days later, Leicester claimed that he was too drunk to know what he was doing on the night in question, but the Stipendiary handed him three months prison with hard labour. His wife was in court to hear how she would so soon be parted from her new husband.

Birmingham Daily Post 26th November 1874

A Vile Parent

When it was discovered that she was being trained as a beggar, eleven year old Mary Overton of Bloxwich was admitted to the Workhouse at Walsall. Like all those entering the institution she was medically examined, whereupon she was found to be suffering from venereal disease. Shockingly, it was her father who had transmitted the disease to her and he who had been encouraging her to beg.

Fifty nine year old miner William Overton, was brought before the court in July 1869 but the proceedings were halted because the proper procedures had not been followed. Overton was discharged but told that the matter would be further looked into.

Whether Overton ever had to face a court again is not known but his poor daughter was still in the Workhouse almost two years later.

Birmingham Daily Post 6th July 1869
1871 census RG10 piece 2965 folio 170 page 8

Stiff Sentences

Some sentences, especially for minor thefts, can seem very harsh, even by the standards of the day as these cases show.

Thomas Whitehouse was transported for seven years for stealing a shirt, the property of John Ross, Walsall. It was judged a reasonable sentence in 1842 given that he had been previously convicted.

Mary Gallagher, "an old offender" was sentenced to three years penal servitude for stealing a piece of bacon from John Stevenson's shop at Wolverhampton in 1862.

Mary Ann Fullard, a domestic servant employed by Archibald Gun, master of the School of Art at Darlington Street, Wolverhampton was imprisoned for six months for stealing part(!) of an opera cloak and a dish for holding water-colour paints.

Staffordshire Gazette and County Standard 6th January 1842
Birmingham Daily Post 15th October 1862
Birmingham Daily Post 21 March 1870

Murder, Misfortune and Misery

Chapter 5

Forensic science today makes it extremely difficult for a murderer to avoid identification, but in the eighteen hundreds things were very different. Unless there was a confession, a reliable witness or some damning piece of evidence, proving a charge of murder, or any lesser crime for that matter, was extremely difficult. In addition, at a time when cause of death was often difficult to determine, there can be no doubt that many crimes went undetected, many more were never solved and that many innocent people went to the gallows.

Canals, and later railways, provided Britain with the infrastructure on which to build its nineteenth century industry and empire. To those who had had enough of the empire and everything in it, they fulfilled a more prosaic role, offering a convenient and generally more reliable method of exit than the time-honoured knife, rope, poison or leap. The Black Country, with a greater density of rail and canal than almost anywhere else in the country, gave rise to an unenviable number of such suicides.

In addition to those who died by their own hand or at the hands of others, we take a look at more reports of accidents and of some people who met an unusual or unlucky demise.

Show-Stopper

James Walford, a showman, committed suicide at Wednesbury in spectacular fashion. He climbed a wall and threw himself from the top of it into a disused mineshaft. As the shaft was filled with noxious gases, it took several days before his ragged body could be recovered. Walford had been acting strangely since an accident seven months beforehand.

Manchester Evening News 6th June 1899

Sadistic Wife-Beater

At the time of the 1871 census Rowland Cooper was a widowed coal miner lodging at Parliament Street, Bilston. Two years later he married Lucy Goodwin, who was about 20 years his junior, but within a little over a year he had sadistically beaten her to death.

On Saturday 2nd May Cooper thrashed his wife twice with a strap and was heard to say that he would kill her if he had to do so again. On the following Tuesday, neighbours heard the pair quarrelling and one witness later saw them arguing in their yard. Cooper was seen to strike his wife twice between the shoulder blades and to kick her before going back into the house.

When she tried to re-enter the house, he came out and dragged her back inside by her hair. Some reports suggest that Cooper now beat his wife with a poker and beat her over the heart with a rolling pin. Whatever form this brutal attack took, she reappeared after a little while, sat down on the doorstep and very soon passed away.

Although there were marks of violence on her body, medical reports showed that the cause of death was suffocation due to her lungs operating at only one fifth of their normal capacity. This was attributed to the blows she had received to her back.

Cooper, who was not defended at court, was found guilty, sentenced to 15 years penal servitude and died ten years later.

Staffordshire Sentinel 23rd July 1874
Western Mail 7th May 1874
Birmingham Daily Post 23th July 1874
Worcestershire Chronicle 1st August 1874
1871 census RG10 piece 2953 folio 17 page 30

Colliery Killer

Forty four year old John Farnall was head engineer at the Wyrley Cannock Colliery Company near Walsall. One of his subordinates, 21 year old James Allsop, had a poor timekeeping record and was often drunk when he arrived for work but Farnall had taken him under his wing and was trying to reform his behaviour. Unfortunately that didn't stop Allsop from shooting him at almost point blank range while they were at work in September 1870.

The young man was apparently half an hour late for work on the fateful day and became abusive when Farnall told him off. The matter quickly escalated to an exchange of kicks and blows until finally Allsop stood back, produced a pistol and fired it straight into body of his boss.

The miscreant now threatened those around him with the weapon and made his escape but he was soon pursued by constable Lindop, who finally caught up with him about two miles away. Allsop turned and threatened to shoot the officer and, as Lindop approached, he discharged the weapon. Fortunately the constable just managed to sidestep the shot and make his arrest. According to Lindop the lad did not seem overly concerned about his acts, telling him that that the first bullet was made from lead and that the second shot consisted of small stones.

Farnall died from his injuries at around five o'clock in the afternoon on the day of the shooting. On his death bed he had exclaimed "Oh dear, for that villain to serve me in this way after I have been a father to him".

Witnesses said that Allsop had threatened to shoot several people at the colliery in the weeks leading up to the crime, including Farnall's son. At his trial he was convicted of manslaughter and given ten years penal servitude. Constable Lindop was awarded £20 for his bravery in making the arrest.

Norfolk News 24th September 1870
Nottinghamshire Guardian 23rd September 1870
Manchester Evening News 8th December 1870

Mutual Suffocation

In January 1862, a four year old and his one year old brother, the children of one Edwin Taylor, were found dead in bed at the family home near Kingswinford. The Coroner's inquest, held at the Bridge Inn, Gorsty Bank, came to the conclusion that the children had 'mutually suffocated' each other(!) and a verdict of accidental death was returned. Today, most people are aware of the danger of carbon monoxide poisoning but, in the age of open fires in bedrooms with poor ventilation, there must have been many such cases.

Birmingham Journal 25th January 1862

Oyster Jack

"Oyster Jack", real name John Macantire (or more likely McIntyre), ran a small shop on West Bromwich High Street selling oysters. He had lived with a woman named Ann Marsh for over a decade and they had two children together. In addition, two children from Marsh's previous relationship lived with them. The couple were heavy drinkers and frequently quarrelled until their relationship finally broke down, at which point they agreed that she should leave with the older children, and he would look after the younger two.

Macantire now gave up drink completely and was said to be much more affectionate to his children, James and Jane as a result. One mid-winter Saturday in 1867, about a year after his separation from Marsh, Macantire was working at his shop until about midnight. At home shortly afterwards a neighbour heard Jane call out "Daddy are you coming to bed?" followed by the reply "Yes and I'll bring some fire to warm you".

On the following Monday, two policemen were informed that the family hadn't been out of the house since Saturday night. As the door was locked, the officers obtained a ladder and entered through a first floor window. The room they entered was unfurnished so they made their way to a back bedroom, where they found the bodies of the man and his two children in the same bed. They were lying on their backs, each with foam around the mouth and their skin discoloured. On the floor was a bucket with holes in it, in the manner of a brazier, the bottom third of which was filled with ash. As there was no ventilation in the room, the three had been suffocated by the fumes. The inquest held the following day returned a verdict of accidental death.

Birmingham Journal 26th January 1867

Coke Fumes

An almost identical case to that above occurred at Bratt Street in the same town in 1893. Mr and Mrs Richards and their son had not been seen all day and in the end forced entry was made to their house at 9pm. The family were all found unconscious in bed, probably as a result of fumes from a bucket of coke that they had taken upstairs at bedtime the night before. They were removed to the hospital but had not regained consciousness by midnight.

Liverpool Echo 23rd November 1893

Wound To Death

Thomas Langley, a worker at Edwards edge tool works in Wolverhampton, suffered a horrible fate in January 1881. Like many factories of the time, Edwards' employed a steam driven overhead shaft system which in turn powered individual pieces of machinery through belts and pulleys.

Langley was polishing a spade when his clothing was caught by the band driving his machine. He was whirled around the shaft and completely entangled before the machinery was brought to a stop. He was so badly crushed that every bone in his body seemed to broken.

Staffordshire Sentinel 20th January 1881

Tram Track Terminates Trip

On a Monday morning in April 1893 George Somers, a 29 year old butcher of Hargate Lane, West Bromwich, set off on a cycle trip with his brother John and their friends. At Dudley Port, Somers for some reason found himself on the wrong side of the road and, in trying to cross to the correct side, met with a terrible accident.

John Daniels, the driver of a two horse brake told the subsequent inquest that one of Somer's wheels had caught the tram line and that the unfortunate man was pitched head-first under the feet of the horses. George was admitted to the district hospital at quarter past ten, but had suffered such extensive head injuries that by six in the evening he was dead.

Birmingham Daily Post 6th April 1893

Murder At 'The Barracks'

'The Barracks' was the name commonly given to a group of around eight houses surrounding a wide courtyard on Bilston Street, Wolverhampton. In July 1863, a couple who made their living manufacturing and selling iron skewers, moved in to one of the houses. They kept themselves to themselves, the man being little seen and the woman obsessively locking her front door even when leaving the house for just a few seconds.

After a couple of weeks, the woman locked up the property, leaving the curtains closed, and told a neighbour that should anyone ask, she was going to the country. A few days later a woman from Willenhall arrived at the Barracks wishing to see her son, Mr Williams, supposedly the rarely-seen husband, and tenant of the locked up house. As there was no-one home, she asked a neighbour to ask Mr Williams to write to his mother when he returned.

The property remained empty until mid-August and in the intervening period, neighbours had noticed a very unpleasant smell in the courtyard. Eventually, when a group of three female neighbours decided they would like to see what was left inside the house, one of them produced a key and they let themselves in.

The house was clearly the source of the noxious smell and in the bedroom they were met with a hideous sight. The horribly mutilated body of Williams lay on a mattress covered with a sheet. It was black with decay and full of maggots. It seemed that tar had also been poured over the body and lay on the floor all around, mixed with blood.

A few days after this grisly find, the body of a woman was discovered in a recently rented property at Dudley. She had apparently died from a substantial dose of Laudanum which, judging by the label on the bottle, had been purchased in Bilston. A bonnet, which was found to be that worn by the woman who had left 'The Barracks', hung from a skylight near the corpse.

The woman had told a neighbour that she was the wife of a lamp-lighter, William Smith, but no other clue to her identity was forthcoming. A verdict of 'Found dead' was all that the inquest jury could return in the case of the body at the Barracks.

Chelmsford Chronicle 21st August 1863

Drowned In The Backyard

When friends of twelve year old John Rushton of Beale Street, West Bromwich, noticed that he had gone missing, a search of the area around his house was begun immediately. His body was shortly discovered in a cistern in the backyard of the house. Many old houses had these underground water tanks, which could hold as much as 1,000 gallons of rainwater, to give an independent supply for washing and so forth. That at Beale Street was surrounded by a knee high wall and had such a narrow opening, that those who saw it, found it hard to understand how the lad had managed to squeeze through the gap.

Birmingham Daily Post 26th November 1878

Drowned In The Locks

In June 1888, sixteen year old William Mills was drowned at the Brades Hall locks on the Birmingham Canal, about a mile west of his home at Oak Road, West Bromwich. He had lost his footing, fallen into the lock and was washed down the draw pit underneath an empty boat; a position from which there was no escape. By the time lock-keeper Thomas Southall managed to retrieve the young man, it was too late.

Gloucester Citizen 12th June 1888

Buried In Hot Cinders

William Stockton, a boy employed at Sparrow's blast furnaces, Stow Heath, Bilston suffered a dreadful accident on 19th March 1870. A large quantity of hot cinder fell on him mangling and burning his body before he could be rescued.

Birmingham Daily Post 21st March 1870

Lethal Cat-Scarer

George Gannaway, a tailor of Darlington Street, Wolverhampton, possessed a six chamber revolver. On 18th August 1887 he had been using it to shoot at cats that had been keeping him awake at night! He left the gun, with one chamber still loaded, under the counter in his shop but put the safety catch on and warned his 13 year old son, George Leonard, not to mess with it.

Inevitably, later in the day when his father was absent, the boy got the gun and started playing with it. He aimed it at another boy who worked in the shop and pulled the trigger but it was set to an empty chamber. The terrified shop-boy dodged the expected bullet and then heard George say "Now, you see me shoot myself". He put the gun to his head, pulled the trigger and fell to the floor stone dead.

Derby Daily Telegraph 19th August 1887

Wanted Man Wanted No More

Joseph Edward Beards, a plater by trade, threw himself in front of a Great Western goods train at Wolverhampton in September 1884 and was decapitated. He had been drinking heavily and had three warrants against him for different offences.

Portsmouth Evening News 14th September 1894

Dragged To His Death

John Brawn, a farmer and 'lime-master' of the Mellish Road, Walsall was returning from the Crown Hotel at Lichfield at around 5pm on a winter evening in 1884, when he was thrown from his gig. His brother Samuel followed along the same road shortly afterwards and, when he reached his gate, he learned of John's accident and was told that his injured brother had been taken to the nearby Cottage Spring Inn.

Samuel went to the inn and, not thinking his brother too badly injured, helped him to his trap and proceeded to take him home. On the way, John told how a group of wagoners had driven past him at high speed and collided with his wheel. Soon after, a man who had previously annoyed him also raced passed and narrowly avoided a second collision.

He told his brother he was shaken and now proceeded with extreme care and at low speed, with his wheels in the well-formed ruts in the road. When he reached Shelfield however, his wheel struck the end of a five inch pipe that had been so arranged as to conduct water from the channels onto nearby land. His horse at first obeyed the call to halt but it then took off unexpectedly, throwing him from the gig.

Unfortunately, his leg became entangled in the wheel causing it to lock, but the horse ran on for another 200 yards. With his head banging on the ground, John struggled until he was able to grab the spokes to raise himself and cry out for the horse to stop. After he was extricated the horse and cart ran on further still, to the Midland Railway bridge in Rushall Road, where it was stopped by a baker's cart.

As soon as Samuel got his brother home he called for medical help, but despite the attention of three medical men over the next two days, the extensive injury inflicted upon his knee joint and leg, claimed his life.

At the conclusion of the inquest, the coroner was asked to make arrangements for the pipe that had caused the accident to be removed, and the police were asked to issue a warning to those who had driven their vehicles so recklessly out of Lichfield.

Birmingham Daily Post 12th December 1884

The West Bromwich Murder Mystery

Robert Spencer was a thirty year old druggist with a shop at High Street, West Bromwich who had been in a relationship for a couple of years with Elizabeth Annie Evans of Victoria Street. Although they had no formal plans to become engaged, Spencer would often visit his girlfriend at her parents home as well as them being together at his premises.

In the spring of 1885 Elizabeth was unwell with gastritis and visited a local doctor, who found that she was also between five and six months pregnant. Very soon after this, around Good Friday, she disappeared. The following week she sent two letters to her mother, but thereafter, nothing more was heard from her.

It later transpired that Elizabeth had gone to the home of a forty year old woman, Sarah Clancey at 57 Dudley Road, West Bromwich, for the purpose of having an abortion. Mrs Clancey 'operated' on the poor woman and Spencer visited several times over the next few days but things did not go to plan, partly because of Elizabeth's' already poor health, and by Wednesday she was dead.

Clancey's husband now took the opportunity to blackmail Spencer, threatening to bring the body to his shop! Initially he helped himself to £20 in 'hush money' from Spencer's cash box, but over the next few years he extorted over £200.

Clancey had buried Elizabeth's body in their garden but upon receiving notice to leave the house about six months later, he dug up the body, burned it in the cellar and then re-buried it.

By the early 1890's Spencer had married and moved his business to Birmingham. Mr Clancey had deserted his wife and children and gone to America and his wife was living at Kingswinford. When a quantity of human bones from Dudley Road were passed to the police, they visited Mrs Clancey in the course of their investigations and found a locket and chain that had belonged to the dead woman.

Furthermore, a woman named Celest Waldron came forward as a witness. She had lodged with the Clanceys at Dudley Road and had been comforting Elizabeth when she died. She was fooled by them into thinking that the body had been taken away by a doctor, or relatives, for a funeral. Crucially, at the trial she stated that she had seen the red dress that Elizabeth was wearing when she disappeared, hanging in the room where she died.

A boy named Wallace Eales who worked at Spencer's shop told how he had seen the Clanceys come to the shop and talk privately to his employer, often taking away goods that weren't accounted for in the ledgers.

In the end, Sarah Clancey's statement made it clear that Spencer, who had shown shock and remorse after the death, was no more than an accessory after the fact. As a result he received a comparatively light two year sentence, whereas she was sentenced to fifteen years.

The letters that could have shed light on Elizabeth's disappearance eight years earlier, had been burned by her father (who had himself died by the time of the trial) because they made his wife cry each time she read them.

Birmingham Daily Post 30th March 1893

Birmingham Daily Post 27th April 1893
Liverpool Echo 28th July 1893

Bodies in The Lake

As was his habit, late one summer evening in July 1845, the mayor of Walsall, Mr J. H. Harvey went for a swim, although this time he did not return. He left his gold watch, a substantial amount of money and his gloves with the rest of his clothes beside the pool known as 'The Lakes', now a part of Walsall Arboretum. The pool was known to be of considerable depth as it was formerly an open-cast limestone working but had fallen into disuse through flooding.

It was supposed that thirty five year old Harvey, a practising local attorney, had been stricken with cramp and unable to reach the shore. In the hunt for the Mayor's body a second man, a saddler named James Oakley, fell into the water and was also drowned.

Two days later the mayor's body had still not been recovered, so a message was sent to London to obtain the help of a specialist diver, who arrived the same day. On the second day of searching, the body rose to the surface of it's own accord and was recovered. An inquest was held immediately and returned a verdict of accidental death.

Whether or not the body of poor Oakley was ever recovered is not known.

Leicestershire Mercury 19th July 1845

A Wave Of Fire

William Hall and Richard Williams died as a result of an accident at the Darlaston Green furnaces in 1869. It was one o'clock on a Sunday morning when the pair were showered in a mass of molten cinder. When Thomas Evans, a furnace labourer, heard a slight explosion, he ran to the casting house and found Hall crawling away from the furnace on his hands and knees and Williams standing upright - both were horribly burned.

After investigation it was thought that the accident had happened because the furnace had been under-used for six shifts during the week. As a result, some mineral had cooled, causing it to harden slightly and 'hang' in the furnace. When the temperature had increased again, this mass of hanging mineral suddenly fell some nine feet, and caused the molten cinder and fire below to spill out over the dam into the casting house where the men were working.

The men were admitted to hospital but both were so badly burned that neither survived until the following day.

Birmingham Daily Post 28th May 1869

Bad Day At The Races

A man who was believed to have lost a substantial amount of money at Chester races on Saturday 14th May 1881, took his life on the way home. When his train reached the vicinity of Albrighton near Wolverhampton, he threw himself from the train.

An engine was despatched from Wolverhampton to investigate, but as it drew near the scene the man was seen to crawl away and put his head on the metals of the opposite track, upon which a train was approaching. His remains were taken to Wolverhampton for identification.

Manchester Courier and Lancashire General Advertiser 17th May 1881

Unresolved Murder At Wednesbury

A heinous murder took place near the junction of the Bilston and Darlaston Roads at Wednesbury in 1869 but the perpetrator was never brought to justice. The victim, Eliza Bowen was a promiscuous woman who had been seen drinking with 42 year old William Hall at various public houses and the Green Dragon Concert Hall in Wednesbury, on the night of Saturday 27th February.

They were also alleged to have been seen together in Mud Lane near the place of her death in the early hours. Her body was discovered around seven thirty the next morning and she appeared to have been dragged off the road and assaulted in a field beside a colliery pit 'bank'.

Her shawl had been twisted around her neck and her bonnet pulled up under her chin. Her clothing was rucked up and her underclothes soiled and torn. Death was due to more than a dozen pieces of iron cinder having been inserted into her body.

A fragment of a scarf found near the body, which it was alleged matched one owned by Hall, was never produced at the inquest and, as there also seemed to be only one positive identification of Hall, the inquest jury was split 8 versus 4 when it was adjourned.

The inquest was resumed with a depleted jury as one member was unable to attend. Hall did not appear at the resumed inquest and could not be compelled by law to do so. The witnesses were all interviewed once more but nothing new came to light and the inquest was adjourned yet again, with the case to be heard at the next Stafford Assizes.

According to various newspapers, the bill committing Hall for trial at the assizes was thrown out, as it was decided that it would be impossible to prove the guilt of any individual.

Sheffield Daily Telegraph 13th March 1869
Liverpool Mercury 29th May 1869
Birmingham Daily Post 28th May 1869
Sheffield Daily Telegraph 22nd July 1869

A Sad Case

At her trial, the case of Sarah Elizabeth Gould was described in court as "an exceedingly sad one, however looked at".

Sarah was a twenty year old single woman with an illegitimate year-old baby named Alfred John. She had been an orphan since the age of 13 and, like many women who found themselves in similar circumstances, she had spent time in the Workhouse, in this case the one on Hallam Street at West Bromwich.

She left the Workhouse for the last time on Monday 7th June with her sister Amelia Goodwin, and went to Amelia's house at Oldbury. The following day they visited Dartmouth Park, where Sarah tried to persuade Amelia to take the child but she declined.

On the evening of following day, Sarah and her baby were at the Albion Hotel, Paradise Street, where the 'boots' John Hatton, who had known her for a couple of years, served her a half pint of ale. Afterwards he walked her to the tram stop at Moor Street, where she intended to catch the 10 o'clock tram back to her sisters house, but the tram was full and she could not get a seat. She was seen around eleven o'clock in Paradise Street by an acquaintance, Jemima Parkes, but no longer had the child with her. She asked if she could stay at Parkes' house that night as she did not wish to return to her sister's, but was refused.

In reality, she could not return to her sister's house because she had murdered the child by drowning it in the canal. The child's body, wearing clothing with the workhouse stamp, was recovered from near middle lock,

Spon Lane, on the Friday of that week, and identified by a member of the Workhouse. Gould was arrested on the following Saturday at Braybrook Street, West Bromwich, and admitted killing the child because she "had no home to go to". She was committed to trial and in December found guilty of wilful murder. She was sentenced to death despite a recommendation for mercy.

Birmingham Daily Post 14th June 1892
Manchester Courier and Lancashire General Advertiser 16th December 1892

Battered To Death

Nearly thirty years before the sad tale of Sarah Gould outlined above, a similar murder took place at Wolverhampton, in September 1866. In this case, 22 year old Mary Brown gave birth in the union workhouse and left less than two weeks later, with a basket containing her few possessions, including some coloured muslin and a pillowcase.

When she was arrested for theft the very next day, she had no child with her. It wasn't until some three weeks later that two men discovered the body of a female child, with it's skull completely battered-in, under a pile of broken bricks and stones in Lear Lane. The body was badly decomposed but still dressed in workhouse clothing and wrapped in the pillowcase and muslin owned by Brown.

Brown had been seen in the vicinity and had even admitted killing the baby to several people although she denied having beaten-in it's skull.

The inevitable verdict was again accompanied by a plea for leniency but she too was sentenced to death at Stafford Assizes.

Chester Chronicle 8th December 1866

Mental Illness

At his trial for the murder of his sweetheart Susannah Jones, 31 year old metal roller William Fryer was found not guilty on the grounds of insanity. It seems that mental illness was prevalent in his family, as his sister was in an asylum and his mother was judged insane when she died, although his brother James was of sound mind.

During the inquest at the Wellington Inn, Park Lane, Tipton, Fryer told those assembled that he had put her in the canal but had also tried to get her out again and nearly drowned himself in the process. He said that he didn't know what he was doing at the time and a witness stated that Fryer had previously complained of burning pains in his head. Another witness, a former landlady, said that he had also tried to hang himself and his superior at work said that Fryer was strange in his ways. Fryer himself was heard to say that it wouldn't have happened if they had put him away sooner.

The inquest heard there was no logical motive for the crime; the young woman was not pregnant and had not been assaulted or robbed. At his trial, it emerged that Fryer was walking along beside the canal with his arm around the girl's waist, when he suddenly pushed her in. A surgeon certified in court that Fryer suffered from an impulsive mania.

Worcester Journal 4th February 1882 & 6th May 1882

Barber Enraged By Rumour

At around 10:30 on a Sunday night in April 1882, Arthur Pearce, a twenty nine year old barber, confronted twenty six year old glass works labourer, Philip Sutherland, at the entry to the house where he was lodging in West Bromwich. In front of a couple of onlookers, Pearce claimed that Sutherland had been spreading rumours about him and a married woman, Mrs Hannah Dickenson, with whom he lodged.

After very brief argument Pearce lost his temper and landed three punches on Sutherland, one of which hit him behind the left ear, causing him to collapse.

As Pearce was making his way back from the fight at 354 Spon Lane, to his house at number 249, he passed Constable Davidson who had heard the commotion and Pearce told him what had happened.

Davidson continued to the scene and helped carry Sutherland into his lodgings. As the man was still unconscious he called a local doctor but Sutherland expired before the doctor arrived.

Officer Davidson later arrested Pearce who, although he had already told him of the assault, said that he had no intention of killing the man. The outcome of any trial is not known, but by 1891 Pearce was lodging with Lois Maxwell, a widowed hairdresser, in Birmingham.

Worcester Journal 6th May 1882

Drowned For Two Pound

Margaret Budd took her own life and that of her youngest child in October 1855, leaving her husband Joseph, an iron puddler, to bring up their two older children. By all accounts the couple had not been very happily married due to her spendthrift ways. The final straw came after she had spent £2 and, to prevent her husband finding out, tried to borrow the money from a friend.

When the loan was not forthcoming, Margaret left home with their two year old child and they were not seen alive again. Two days later, when their bodies were recovered from the canal near the Brunswick Ironworks at Lea Brook, Wednesbury, she still had the child clasped in her arms.

Staffordshire Sentinel and Commercial & General Advertiser 6th October 1855

Accidentally Poisoned Himself

Thomas Gibson, a 36 year old surgeon with a wife and six children, lived and practised at Paradise Street, West Bromwich. Gibson hadn't been in particularly good health and was said to be suffering from 'congestion of the brain' during the months leading up to his death on Thursday 22nd September 1864.

On that day he had sent his assistant Edward Woodward for some brandy to help with his condition. A patient came in shortly after and Gibson once again sent his pupil out, this time for some Laudanum to treat the woman. He obtained the drug from the nearby High Street chemist William Bullus, although it was dispensed by his brother Benjamin. The Laudanum was in a bottle labelled 'Tincture Opii' but it did not carry a 'Poison' label.

After delivering the drug to his master, Woodward was sent out yet again for brandy. During this third errand Gibson drank a small quantity of the Laudanum by mistake thinking it to be the original bottle of brandy. When Woodward returned Gibson asked him what was in the bottle that he had drunk from and Woodward replied "Tincture Opii".

Gibson now recognised the danger he was in and gave instructions as to how he should be kept from falling asleep by being walked around, splashed with water and given coffee. Despite the prompt attendance of Bullus and the administration of some other drug (presumably a stimulant), by the time another doctor could be summoned it was too late.

The inquest, held at the nearby White Horse Inn, returned a verdict that precisely reflected the reason for Gibson's demise. Bullus received a reprimand for not labelling the fatal bottle as poison, and Woodward for leaving the bottle within Gibson's reach when his master was already under the effects of alcohol.

Birmingham Daily Post 24th September 1864
1861 census RG09 piece 2031 folio 73 page 23

Stairway To Heaven

John Merrick, a forty four year old ironworker, lodged at Cliffords Buildings, Pelsall. One Sunday in 1889 he had been drinking heavily and went to bed early. The next morning he left home early but returned a few hours later. On his way back upstairs he stumbled and remarked to Mrs Astbury, his landlady, "I shall break my ____ neck before I've finished". Coming downstairs a little while later he fell from the top step to the very bottom where he was found to have died as a result of a broken neck.

Birmingham Daily Gazette 5th July 1889

Fatal Playtime

Thomas Ellis was a thirteen year old boy employed at the Patent Shaft works at Wednesbury in 1864. He and some other employees of similar age were playing in a yard at the works when a sixteen hundredweight log fell from a stack on which he was climbing. The timber landed across his head and chest, killing him outright.

A verdict of accidental death was returned with no sanction against the company.

Birmingham Daily Post 24th September 1864

Murder And Suicide At Home

The body of 55 year old Eliza Hall was found in her locked bedroom at 31 Herbert Street, West Bromwich. She was a live-in housekeeper for Edwin Hassall, a building contractor who was just a year older.

His son, Major Hassall, had returned from work at ten in the morning to find the house quiet and exactly as he had left it at 6am, which was very unusual. As the housekeeper didn't respond to calls or knocking at the door of her room, the Major and his brother Alfred obtained a ladder so as to look through her first floor window. Greeted by a most distressing sight they at once called the police.

Sergeant Owen arrived forthwith, broke down the bedroom door and found Hall lying across the foot of the bed. There was a considerable amount of blood on the bed as her throat had been cut but no weapon was to be seen.

The officer now proceeded to Hassall's bedroom, which was on the same floor, where he found the man lying face down beside the bed in a pool of blood. His chest was bare and beside the body lay a large carving knife. It seemed that Hassall had killed his housekeeper then took his own life.

In his evidence to the inquest, held at the local Law Courts, Major Hassall said that Mrs Hall was probably stronger than his father but could have been surprised by being attacked from behind as she was quite deaf. The inquest heard from Dr Manley that she could not have inflicted the injury herself and that an attack from behind was consistent with the injuries to her hands.

Hassall stated that their father had been acting strangely since being injured in a gas explosion at home some 18 months earlier. He had been rather depressed about his business, which was not as good as he would have liked, and the death of a third son just five weeks beforehand. His odd behaviour had been noted by people in the street and members of a bible class that he attended.

Mr Hassall and his housekeeper had always got on well together, but she was due to leave his employment on the day of the tragedy because of his strange behaviour. According to witnesses they had only ever had petty quarrels, and he had never threatened her or anyone else or talked of suicide. Although he had been depressed and seemingly under a great burden, no-one suspected that he might be at all dangerous.

The inquest touched on matters of Mr Hassall's will and insurance but there were no issues that indicated that a third party might have a motive for his murder. In the end, the inquest jury decided that Hassall was guilty of the murder of his housekeeper and that he committed suicide while in a state of temporary insanity.

Birmingham Daily Post 16th June 1894

Outrage At Wednesbury

The word 'Outrage' often appears in nineteenth century newspaper headlines, sometimes to indicate murder but most often to indicate crimes of a sexual nature. In this case it was used to indicate the latter when it appeared in the headline: "Outrage, Arson and Suicide".

Thomas Stevenson, a 40 year old labourer, was known as a hard-working, honest and sober man who lived in a small cottage at Vicar Street, Wednesbury.

Things were not as they seemed however, since his 16 year old daughter had determined to take out a warrant against him for rape. At 8am on the day she intended to obtain the warrant, flames were seen coming from the cottage and the fire proceeded to consume most of the building before it was put out.

In the ruins, Stevenson's body was found with his throat slit and an open razor beside the corpse. The police also recovered two letters, one addressed to Stevenson's daughter, the other to a printer. The inquest, where the evidence was said to be of an immoral and revolting nature, returned a verdict that Stevenson had taken his own life while of unsound mind.

Note: The newspaper reports variously state The Vicarage and Vicarage Lane as the address but the 1871 census lists his address as 3, Vicar Street which is off Vicarage Road. The young woman may have been his step-daughter Sarah Bardell (16) rather than his daughter Elizabeth (12)

> Manchester Courier and Lancashire General Advertiser 1st April 1876
> Manchester Evening News 30th March 1876
> 1871 census RG10 piece 2987 folio 68 page 9

Wednesbury Wheat Murder

An inquest into the death of a baby was held at the Scott's Arms Inn, Kings Hill, Wednesbury in January 1859. The female child had been dead for some weeks but seemed to have been delivered at full term and was of average size and weight. The body had been found in a nearby privy and the cause of death was a quantity of wheat ears and straw that had been forced into the child's mouth and throat causing suffocation.

Following up local information, Sergeant Samuel Went interviewed Mary Davis who he suspected as being the mother of the child, but she denied ever having been "in the family way". Next he went to see Mary's mother, Rebecca Davis. On examining a bed at her home, he discovered a stain which he thought may have been caused during childbirth, but she claimed that it had been caused by contact with a rusty bedstead.

In a closet, the officer discovered a substantial quantity of wheat, although Davis had earlier claimed she had none in the house. She also denied that her daughter had been with child but Sergeant Went did not believe her, and arrested both of them on suspicion of murder.

In the end the inquest jury returned a verdict of wilful murder, by person or persons unknown, as the evidence against the two women was deemed very suspicious but inconclusive.

The Standard 14th January 1859
Manchester Times 22nd January 1859

Died Delivering Supper

One cold and foggy night in February 1881, Abraham Dyke was sent to a Wednesbury colliery with his father's supper, but he never returned from the errand. His body was found at the bottom of an embankment, with his face severely bruised and his eyes and ears partially eaten away by rats. It was supposed that the poor lad had lost his way, fallen down the embankment and died from exposure.

Lancaster Gazette 5th February 1881

Bathing In The Cut

The canal at Lea Brook claimed another life 11 years after those of Margaret Budd and her child outlined earlier in this chapter, although this time, suicide was not intended. Fifteen year old Theodore John Morris had been bathing in the canal when he got out of his depth, and presumably being unable to swim, lost his life. His body was recovered three quarters of an hour later, the coroner's inquest returned a verdict of accidental death.

Birmingham Daily Post 14th June 1866

Tragedy At Swan Village

Isaac Turner took his own life on his eighteenth birthday, Sunday 11th August 1889.

He had been working as a horse-driver at Sandwell Park Colliery but had recently lost his job. On Wednesday 7th he had pawned some of his clothes in order to buy a rail ticket to Nottingham, where his sister lived, ostensibly to look for work.

By Saturday he was back in West Bromwich. where he made arrangements to lodge at the home of Sarah Pearce of Glue Yard, Lower High Street. He told Sarah that he had walked all the way from Lichfield and was very tired, saying he should have to give up rambling and make himself content at home instead.

In his testimony to the inquest, Isaac's father Frank said that his son had been acting strangely and was off his food. He had seen Isaac on Saturday and again on Sunday, when his son was talking to some men in a field, but didn't approach him. The coroner expressed great surprise at this, given his son's odd behaviour. Frank Turner also identified a piece of newspaper on which Isaac had written "Dear Friends, I am going to commit suicide on the railway at Black Lake".

Isaac's mother, Nancy, said that her son was back at home at Kings Street, Guns Lane, on Sunday but seemed to be "put about over something" and complained of feeling unwell. She said he had a sweetheart, but as far as she knew, nothing untoward had happened between them. In response to the coroner's probing for an explanation of the father's conduct she called her son "a very stupid boy" to which the coroner retorted "and the father was equally stupid".

George Henry Williams, a porter, said he found Isaac's body on the railway on Sunday night, the head having been completely severed. The jury returned a verdict of "suicide while in a state of temporary insanity".

Birmingham Daily Post 16th August 1889

Fatal Fight

John Shore and James Wardle had been drinking for most of the day at the Bird In Hand beer-house in Wednesbury during the Wake. At around 5pm they had an argument about a threepenny bet and Shore vowed that if Wardle would not pay he would "punch it out of him".

The two men left the premises and stripped off their shirts in the yard in preparation for a fight. The publican rushed outside to persuade the men not to fight, but they jumped over his wall into a field, followed by a group of onlookers, where they again squared up against one another. The publican intervened once more but he was pulled off by some of the others present and went back to his business.

Jabez Rubery of Darlaston was returning from West Bromwich when he saw the men in the field and, as he knew both of them, stopped his horse to see what was happening. Within a matter of minutes Shore had received a blow to the side of his head which caused him to collapse and very soon to expire. Wardle absconded immediately and at the time of the inquest had not been traced. The jury returned a verdict of manslaughter against him in his absence.

Staffordshire Advertiser 14th September 1839

Drowned At Walsall

An inquest held at the Globe Inn, James Bridge, into the death of sixteen year old Thomas Drury of Old Pleck Road, Walsall returned a verdict of accidental death. He had gone to bathe in the canal with a number of friends on the evening of 4th July 1889 but got out of his depth and drowned.

Birmingham Daily Gazette 5th July 1889

Fratricide and Attempted Suicide

Brothers Ernest (22), Thomas(17) and John Harper(15) shared a bedroom at the Victoria Inn, Poultney Street, Wolverhampton, where their father was the landlord. Since leaving the Navy around the end of 1887, Ernest had quarreled with his brothers a few times, but in general all three got on well together.

One morning in April 1888, Ernest got up very early and went into his parents bedroom but was told to go back to bed by his mother. Within seconds of returning to his room there was terrible screaming and the sounds of a violent struggle. Mr Harper dashed to the room where he was met with a shocking sight - Thomas lay on his blood-soaked bed with his head almost completely severed, while John was struggling to defend himself from Ernest, who was wielding a knife with a 15 inch blade. Before their father could take any action, Ernest threw himself through a window and landed head-first on the street below.

Although suffering a serious head injury, when asked why he had attacked his brother, Ernest was just able to utter "Don't know". He was described as of weak intellect and occasionally subject to periods of despondency but had never shown any sign of violence before. It was supposed that he had attacked his brother in his sleep although he had fetched the knife from downstairs.

Western Mail 1st May 1888

Pushed To His Death

William Hampton was charged with the manslaughter of Benjamin Butler, a twenty nine year old miner, at Wednesbury. Butler was a married man and had been staying with his father during the Wednesbury Wake* in 1838.

At around 11pm on 8th May, Benjamin was sitting on a wall near his father's house, situated between Wednesbury and Darlaston, talking to his sister who stood nearby. The wall was just two feet high on the pavement side but there was a five foot drop behind it.

The accused and two other men were passing on the opposite side of the street when Hampton suddenly crossed the road, walked up to Butler and pushed him off the wall. He glanced over the wall and saw Butler lying on the ground below, crossed the road back to his companions and they then ran off.

At the trial various witnesses were called but none could offer a motive for Hampton's actions. Butler's sister Sarah, in response to one claim, said that her brother had not insulted Hampton and his friends or called out "does your mother know you're out?".

After the incident Butler was carried into the house by his father but remained unconscious until seven the next morning. Mr Dickenson, the surgeon who was called to attend to him, said that Butler had been revived by a warm bath but when able to talk said he could not feel his arms or legs. From this the doctor inferred that he had a spinal injury to the third or fourth vertebrae. He remained conscious until his death at 2pm.

A distant relation of Butler's said he was walking near Hampton and a friend as they crossed the churchyard the following day when he heard him say " I threw a man over a wall last night, I don't know whether he is dead or not and I'm damned if I care".

The judge in his summing up said that the county, and Wednesbury and Darlaston in particular, were known for acts of a barbarous and wanton nature. He said it deserved to be generally known that if a man had died as a result of another man's act of wantonness, he would be transported for life. In this case he did not believe that Hampton intended to kill or even harm Butler but a sentence of one year with hard labour would serve as a salutary lesson that would remain with him for the rest of his life.

*It was probably the May cattle fair as the main Wake was held in September.

Staffordshire Advertiser 21st July 1838

In Search Of A Dowry

In December 1841 three thieves broke in to the house of Matthew Adams at Delves Bank, Walsall through the roof of his pantry. They had somehow discovered that Mr Adams had saved £100 as a 'marriage portion' for his daughter and was keeping it at his house.

Mr Adams, a man of more than seventy years of age, was woken by the noise and went to investigate. As he opened the door and confronted the three men, one of them took up a hammer and dealt him two powerful blows to the head that killed him outright.

A woman who lived next door heard the commotion and opened a window to see what was happening. She saw the three men at Mr Adams' house, one of whom threw a stone at her to drive her back inside. As the men fled the alarm was raised, and a group of 'navvies' who lived nearby set off in pursuit but they were too far behind to catch up.

A pistol was discovered at the house, evidently dropped by one of the assailants, and when Superintendent Raymond of the Walsall Police began to make enquiries, he was told of a young man named Boswell who had often been seen firing a percussion-cap pistol in the area. The following morning Raymond and a constable went to interview Boswell and found him at home having breakfast with his mother.

When shown the pistol, Boswell denied all knowledge of it and said that his gun was still at home and he accordingly showed it to the officers. Despite this Boswell was taken into custody and the pistol from the crime scene taken to a gun-lock maker for examination. When disassembled it was found that the main spring of the lock had been recently replaced.

Raymond now took the gun to another gun-lock maker, in Park Street, who was able to identify the weapon as one he had repaired some three weeks earlier, and to confirm that Boswell was the owner.

While in custody, Boswell seemed to further imply his guilt by trying to escape. He had somehow obtained the blade of an awl, which he used to chip away at the mortar between the bricks of his cell. He had managed to remove three bricks before the attempted jailbreak was discovered.

In the end it was found to be one of Boswell's companions, seventeen year old Joseph Wilkes, who was guilty of the murder and, at the Assizes in March, he was sentenced to hang. He had brutally caved-in the skull of an old man and forfeited his own life for nothing, as the three young intruders had left empty handed.

Staffordshire Gazette and County Standard 9th December 1841
Worcester Journal 24th March 1842

Strangled Her Child

Sarah Jane Kendrick (formerly Bache) was charged with the wilful murder of her daughter on 1st May 1895. On the afternoon of the previous day, a neighbour suspected something was not right at the Kendrick household in Walsall and, having gained entry, found the woman sitting on a bed moaning and repeating "We have done it". Beside her lay the body of her daughter who had been strangled. She had been acting strangely since the child was born about three months earlier; perhaps the crime was a result of what we now recognise as post-natal depression.

She was committed for trial but whether it ever took place is unknown, as there are passing references to her state of mind in reports of another case in July 1895. Her husband Walter Frank Kendrick, a leather currier, was living as a single man at Station Street at the time of the 1901 census.

Worcestershire Chronicle 4th May 1895
RG13 piece 2701 folio 79 page 39
Lichfield Mercury 26th July 1895
Derby Mercury 31st July 1895

Addendum

The following lists may be useful to genealogists and local historians. The first is a list of surnames mentioned in this book and the second is a list of streets, businesses and so forth organised by town. Some of these streets no longer exist, while others may have been renamed. Similarly, many business, public houses and organisations will have ceased to exist or been absorbed into larger concerns. In all cases, spellings have been copied verbatim from the original newspaper reports and may therefore be slightly different to spellings on censuses and elsewhere.

List of Surnames

Adams
Adey
Agers
Allen
Allsop
Arkinstall
Asbury
Atkins
Ayre
Bagot
Bailey
Bannister
Bardell
Bargen
Barrett
Bashford
Bates
Bayley
Beard
Beards

Beech
Bennett
Beston
Bevan
Birch
Bird
Blower
Book
Boswell
Botham
Bowater
Bowen
Bradbury
Bradley
Brawn
Brewer
Brice
Broadbent
Brookes
Brown
Buckstone
Budd
Bullus
Butcher
Butler
Bytheway
Caddick
Cane
Cartwright
Carty
Chatwin
Cheadle
Childs

Clancey
Clark
Clarke
Colclough
Cole
Conolly
Cooper
Cope
Costigan
Cozens
Craddock
Daniels
Darley
Darlington
Davenport
Davidson
Davis
Dean
Dell
Derry
Devaney
Dickenson
Didcott
Didlock
Dight
Drury
Dudley
Durkins
Dyke
Eagles
Eales
Ellis
Evans

Eveson
Farley
Farmer
Farnall
Farren
Farrington
Fenner
Ford
Fox
Foxall
Fryer
Fuel
Fullard
Gallagher
Gannaway
Garner
Gee
Genders
George
Gibbons
Gibson
Godfrey
Golby
Goodwin
Gould
Greenfield
Griffin
Grigg
Grimes
Guest
Hadley
Hall
Hampton

Harper
Harrison
Harvey
Hassall
Hatton
Hawkins
Hayes
Heath
Hill
Hobbins
Hodson
Holden
Holloway
Holt
Howard
Hughes
Hunt
Huntley
Husband
Jackson
James
Jarvis
Jasper
Jenks
Jennings
Johnson
Jones
Keep
Kelly
Kendrick
Killean
King
Knight

Knock
Lake
Lambert
Langley
Lavender
Lawrence
Lemperi
Leonard
Lewis
Lindop
Lockley
Lucas
Lyall
Lycett
Macantire
Malone
Malone
Maloy
Mannion
Marlow
Marsh
Martin
Matthews
Maxwell
McCrohan
McDermott
Meredith
Merrick
Middleton
Mills
Mizen
Moore
Moores

Morris
Morrison
New
Nicholls
Norman
O'Malley
Oakley
Oldbury
Onions
Overton
Owen
Owen
Page
Parker
Parkes
Parton
Pearce
Pearson
Pedley
Pemberton
Perrins
Perry
Phipps
Podmore
Poole
Powell
Pratt
Preston
Proctor
Pugh
Pye
Raymond
Richards

Roberts
Robinson
Rogers
Rose
Rubery
Ruby
Rushton
Russell
Salter
Samuel
Sheepy
Sheldon
Shore
Simms
Simpson
Slim
Smith
Somers
Sparrow
Spencer
Stackhouse
Stanton
Stevenson
Stockton
Sutherland
Tanday
Taylor
Tew
Thacker
Thomas
Thompson
Timmins
Tonge

Tonks
Toy
Turner
Waldron
Walford
Walker
Ward
Wardle
Wayte
Weaver
Whelan
Whitehouse
Wiggins
Wilberry
Wilkes
Williams
Willis
Wilson
Winkle
Winter
Wood
Woodall
Woodward

List of Streets and Businesses

West Bromwich

Albion Hotel (PH)
Barrows Brickworks
Beale Street
Bellevue Gardens, Rood End
Bratt Street
Bromford Lane
Cophall Street
Couse & Bailey
Crookhay Ironworks
Dartmouth Arms Inn (PH)
Dartmouth Park
Davis & Bloomer, West Bromwich
Dudley Port Railway Station
Dudley Road
Glue Yard
Golds Hill
Great Bridge Street
Green Street
Guns Lane
Halford Lane
Hall End Colliery
Hall Street
Hallam Street
Hare & Hounds, Mayers Green (PH)
Hargate Lane
Hateley Heath Colliery
Herbert Street

High Street
Horton & Sons Colliery
John Bethell & Co, West Bromwich
Johnsons Ironworks
Kings Street
Loveday Street
Maria Street
Millfields Colliery
Moor Street
New Street
Oak Road
Old Church
Paradise Street
Prince of Wales Inn (PH)
Pump House Colliery
Robinson Brothers
Royal Exchange
Sandwell Park Colliery
Scotland Passage
Sheepwash Lane
Smith Street
Spon Lane
Swan Colliery
Tantany Colliery
Walsall Street
West Bromwich Railway Station
West Bromwich Workhouse

Wednesbury

Beggars Row
Bescot Railway Station

Bird In Hand (PH)
Bridge Street
Brunswick Ironworks
Burrows Colliery
Camp Street
Coppice Street
Darlaston Green Furnaces
Darlaston Road
Dudley Street
Elwells Pool
George & William Lees Adams
Green Dragon Concert Hall
High Bullen
High Street
Holloway Bank
Holyhead Road
Jolly Brewers Inn (PH)
Kings Hill
Lower Dudley Street
Market Place
Moxley Street
Mud Lane
Old Park Road
Patent Shaft
Queen Street
Ridding Lane
Scott's Arms Inn (PH)
St James Street
St Johns Church
Union Street
United Methodist Free Church
Vicar Street
Wednesbury Oak Colliery

West Bromwich Road
Workhouse Lane

Walsall

Ablewell Street
Birchill Hall Ironworks
Bloxwich Road
Boys & Sons
Boys Timber Merchants
Bradford Street
Bridgeman Street
Burrowes Street
Castle Ironworks
Church Street
Coach & Horses Inn (PH)
Cottage Hospital
Cottage Spring Inn (PH)
Cricket Ball (PH)
Deadman's Lane
Delves Bank
Digbeth
Duignan, Lewis & Lewis
Five Ways
Globe Inn (PH)
Green Lane
Hollyhedge Lane
Hospital Street
Jobbern & Arrowsmith Brickworks
Jones' Ironworks
Lichfield Street
Mellish Road

Navigation Street
New Street
Old Pleck Road
Orlando Street
Paddock Lane
Park Hill Colliery
Park Street
Rising Sun Inn, Bloxwich (PH)
Rushall Street
Rutter Street
Ryecroft Junction
St Georges Theatre
Stafford Street
Station Street
W J Biddow
Walsall Railway Station
Windmill (PH)
Walsall Workhouse
Wyrley Cannock Colliery

Wolverhampton

Bilston Railway Station
Bilston Road
Bilston Street
Bishop Street
Bushbury Junction
Cannock Road
Corn Exchange
Corporation Swimming Baths
Darlington Street
Davis Bros & Co

Dog & Duck Inn
Dudley Street
Edwards Edge Tool Works
Five Ways
Four Ashes Railway Station
Grand Turk Inn
Great Brickkiln Street
Grimstone Street
Hemmingsley & Co
Horseley Fields Tavern
Joseph Bates
Larches Lane, Wolve
Lear Lane
Little Brickkiln Street
Littles Lane
Low Level Station
Lower Stafford Street
North Street
Parliament Street, Bilston
Pipers Row
Poultney Street
Poultney Street
Queen Street
Racecourse
Redman & Co
Salop Street
Shamrock Inn
Snow Hill
Sparrow's Ironworks
Stafford Road Works
Steelhouse Lane
Stewart Street
Temple Street

Victoria Inn
Victoria Street
Warwick Street
William Evans & Son
Workhouse

Printed in Great Britain
by Amazon